Jan

Thank you for being
a true friend to my
mom & me.

Love Lillie,
(Sophie)

Copyright

No part of this book may be reproduced in any form written, electronic, recording or photocopying without written permission of the publisher or author.

Although every precaution has been taken to verify the accuracy of the information contained herein, the author and publisher assume no responsibility for any errors or omission. No liability is assumed for damages that may result from the use of information contained within.

Books may be purchased by contacting the publisher and author at:

lillie@mooofadog.co.uk

www.mooofadog.co.uk

Moo of a dog

Lillie Abbott
BSc (Hons) KCAI CD ABTC ATI TCBTS ISAP

Dedication

For my dad Jim. Whilst he is no longer with us he taught me to always fight for my dreams through hard work and dedication. I hope you would be proud of the person I have become.

For Isobell, Lady, Pippa, Zoe, Honey and Otto for teaching me so much every day you were with me, not a day goes by that I don't think of you all.

For Lazarus, Vier and Itsy, my three beautiful siblings, who whilst not planned have made my life so rich with joy and taught me so much.

For Ezekiel my original Moo of a dog! Whilst you have never been easy you have been my true friend and partner and I look forward to the years to come with you by my side.

To Ignatius, my beautiful little sassy sausage. If we make it through your teens with my sanity intact it will be a miracle!

For Ziggy whilst not mine, I love every moment we shuffle around together, your soul feeds mine,

Acknowledgements

Thank you to my amazing husband Richard for holding me, guiding me and protecting me, always.

To my wonderful friend Munchkin. You have been by my side every step of the way and have spurred me on even when I wanted to quit. Thank you for always believing in me.

Thank you to my Mom Victoria and my Godmother Sally for giving me my love of animals, you gave me such a rich and wonderful childhood.

Thank you to Alison and Mick for being there to listen to me and to encourage me, without your help I wouldn't have had the confidence to even start this book!

Thank you to my wonderful chosen sister Michelle without you by my side for over 30 years I would be in a very different place.

To those reading this book, thank you. You have made my dreams come true!

Contents

I do love the camera!

Foreword

I have been helping and training owners and their dogs for the last 10 years professionally and love every minute of it.

Having had dogs since I was 11, I have dealt with most problems along the way from puppy teeth that feel like your hands are being tattooed, to coming home to no door, table, freezer etc. (it's a long list!)

At present I have five dogs: three German Shepherds x German Pointers - Lazarus, Vier and Itsy; a long coated black German Shepherd - Ezekiel, oh how he has tested my skills! Finally, there is Ignatius our newest family member, a black and tan long haired mini dachshund.

I truly believe we all learn something new from each of our dogs and that has never been truer than now with my big boy Ezekiel. But what a journey we have been on and continue to be on (yep it's true even us professionals find it hard sometimes and have to ask for help, you are not on your own!)

So why am I mentioning this?

The world of Dog Training and Behaviour is at this time unregulated, this means anyone can decide to become a dog trainer or behaviourist and claim to be such.

No qualifications or experience are needed, you can literally start up a business and start teaching others and working with dogs with problem behaviours and no one is there to challenge whether you have the experience, knowledge and qualifications to do this.

This can mean that sadly some can and do set up and work with dogs and their humans who sadly do not have the relevant knowledge, experience of qualifications and this can make matters so much worse let alone dangerous!

So why listen to me and read my book?

Well, yes, I have owned dogs for many years and so can empathise with the struggles you are going through but more than that I have spent more money than I would ever admit to my husband on learning from the best, gaining hands on experience, learning my trade and skills and I continue to learn each and every day.

Anyone who knows me, knows there is never a time when I am not working away on a new qualification, out gaining more experience or off down a rabbit hole learning something new that can help my clients and their dogs to live peacefully together.

I am more than happy for anyone to ask for my credentials and I actively encourage it. After all, would you send your child to school without having first checked if they are safe there and in the knowledge they will learn from their teachers the right way to do things from those with proven knowledge and experience? I very much doubt it. So why do we allow ourselves and our beloved dogs to be trained by someone who hasn't put the time and effort into learning their trade!

My list of credentials below have all been awarded after extensive written and 'in person' assessment. These haven't been a case of just writing a few words and here you go! You have to prove your ability through research, essays and hands-on assessments!

So what are my credentials?

- Kennel Club Accredited Instructor - Companion Dogs
- The Canine Behaviour and Training Society - Full Dog Training Member
- Animal Behaviour and Training Council - Animal Training Instructor
- International Society of Animal Professionals - Full Member
- Canine Behaviour (level 5) awarded with distinction

  So please if you decide to look for a professional dog trainer or behaviourist please, please, please make sure you check and verify their credentials first.
- It literally could save you £'s and even possibly one day your dog's life!

Sleepy pup!

Preface

Before we begin a few quick notes for you to read….

This book is a little different to most.

Part one we are going to look at some of the most annoying and frustrating behaviours I have come across with tenacious teens, these are the ones that I myself have struggled with over the years but also the ones that my clients come to me with the most, it may come across as rather tongue in cheek but it's really not, these are behaviours that can be dangerous to you, others around you and to your dog.

I find it best to just get this out in the open, let it all out, rant, laugh, cry, scream all of it (preferably without the dog in the same room with you, as let's be honest here they don't yet know this isn't the way to behave). Trust me it can be really cathartic to let it all out, there is nothing to be embarrassed about, nothing to worry over we have all been there and we are going to get through this together.

Part two of this book will look over some of the behaviours you may see from your dog when they are trying to communicate with you. Looking at how to recognise them and understand how your dog is feeling is a great step to two way communication with your dog.

Part three will go into some of the struggles you may be having (that honestly most of us with a tenacious teen will see). Whilst perfectly normal for a dog of this age, they can be really frustrating and can make you feel really alone!

Part four and part five we will look at how to deal with those problem behaviours and the exercises you can use to train your dog so that we too can have a chilled out fido in the home and out and about.

This may appear a slightly odd set up for a book, but I find breaking it down and going through each section in turn makes it that little bit easier. First we need to understand our dogs then Motivate, Observe and Optimise your training.

When reading part four and five of the book set out times for you to put the book down and go and try out training exercises with your dog as you go along.

A tenacious teen needs lots of rest, brain work is exhausting for them and training is one of the best ways to tire their brains.

Some simple rules to follow:

Only train for a maximum of three minutes at a time (I find the time it takes for the kettle to boil and the tea bag to infuse is perfect - what can I say I drink earl grey!).

Only train 3 times per day maximum (that's a lot for a young dog and hey who liked homework when they were a teen!)

Make sure your dog has the opportunity to sleep between sessions, at least 30 minutes this will help them to take the learning on board.

Play with your dog, training sessions should always be fun, so before you start training play with your dog even if it's just for a few minutes beforehand, do this again when you finish.

Always make sure their needs have been met before training, so they have been out to the toilet, had a drink, and not ravenously hungry (a little hungry can help so they want to work for their rewards).

Easier said than done, but are you calm in the right frame of mind? (Your dog can tell when you're not and if you are stressed your dog will be too, if now isn't a good time that's fine pick another time just as long as you don't always find an excuse not to train). After all this book is no use to you if you aren't going to put the time and effort it to help your dog understand the rules).

Earoles!

Disclaimer!

I am the first to admit that I have made mistakes, and have messed it up before now. Honestly I have no idea how some of my early dogs turned out to be so well adjusted it was clearly more luck than judgement!

I will also admit that my dogs are not perfect! What they are is perfect for me and that is all I can ask of them and me.

There have been days when I have cried, screamed and laughed all in the space of a few minutes. Days when I have thought my dogs would be better off with someone else, days when I wanted to give it all up, days when I thought I couldn't go on, days when I look at what I am doing with my own dogs and thought, if my clients could see me now!

I swear taking your own advice is the hardest thing to do and to be a dog owner when you have spent years and years learning your trade and learning the science behind it is exhausting! There are no two ways about it, ignorance to an extent really is bliss, but then I look at my dogs now and think thank God I know how to help them and when I don't, I know where to go to get help.

Owning a dog is exhausting! First the puppy stage where you have no sleep, then it feels like all they do is sleep, before you know it you wish they would just go to sleep even for ten minutes. Then before you know it they are a teen, all your hard work appears to have gone out of the window, you are tired, exhausted and quite frankly you have had enough!

"As I am writing this ironically my puppy has just bitten my leg and yep you guessed it I automatically shouted 'NO', I know better, I know this isn't the thing to do but my life it hurts!"

Be kind to yourself, no-one can be perfect all of the time we are all human!

You know or at least you think you do that it will all get better soon, but right now there is no light at the end of the tunnel. You have work early in the morning, your dog has had an accident in the kitchen, you have walked in it with bare feet and to top it off, it's raining outside and you now have to go take them for a walk regardless of the weather, then there is the mud, my life never before have you seen so much mud!

Your tyrannosaurus teen is racing around the house, chewing their way through anything they can get their teeth into, the zoomies are through the roof, on the settee, off the settee, around the lounge, into the kitchen and back off we go again.

You can't eat a meal without being watched, pawed at, jumped up, barked at, the list goes on and on and on.

When will it get easier????

Well, what I can say is put the work in, listen to the advice given in this book and you are on a great path to having a much easier dog to live with. Get a trainer or behaviourist if needed and you will find with a few months of hard work the rest of your lives together will be so much easier.

In all honesty though, how I have survived Ezekiel I will never know, I have learnt so much from him and it is always the more difficult dogs we learn from but oh my he has been a challenge!

Veterinary care

First and foremost, before we go any further let me be crystal clear on one point.

Before you undergo any training or behaviour adjustment with your dog get them checked by a vet!

Dogs do not show pain until they are really, really in pain, even the ones like Ezekiel who are absolute wusses will do everything they can to not show pain.

The majority of cases I have been asked to assist with, in particular where a new behaviour has appeared the dog is in some kind of discomfort or pain.

Awkward teen!

Part One

What is a tenacious teen?

Look mom, I am so clever!

What is a Moo of a dog?

Many years ago I used to work as a farmer (random I know), working with cows taught me how much dogs are so alike to them in their mannerisms.

Cows are immensely clever and if they can find a way around what you want them to do, they will.

They are kind, loyal and loving creatures who have individual personalities and will do pretty much anything for a treat or even better an ear scritch.

That said they can be a right pain too! That's a lot of animal to move if they don't wish to, if they want to head off one way well it's pretty much the case that is the way you are going unless you show them care and respect and ask them to come with you and show them why that is a better option!

They do not respond well to fear or punishment and can become worried and even depressed very easily, let alone dangerous!

Dogs are very similar, years ago we used 'dominance' and would make our dogs do what they needed to do by going 'hands on'. Thankfully this has changed and we now know that positive reinforcement is the way forward, a much kinder relationship built on trust and respect of each other that yields much stronger, long lasting, fear free results.

So when I say do you have a 'moo' of a dog, I am referring to all tenacious teens. Who like their bovine (and human) counterparts, ask questions, push the boundaries, ask 'why' and push every button you have to 'test' if they really need to do something.

These are the dogs I love, the tenacity, the zest for life, the questioning if it is really worth listening to you, making their own decisions (and hopefully always learning from the answers they get, whether this be a lesson we want them to learn or not!).

Ezekiel was and still is the original Moo of a dog, he tested everything!

When he hit his 'teens' he questioned everything!

You want me to sit! What happens if I don't? Oh I don't get paid! Damn it I will sit then, but just this once!

You're calling my name! Nah don't feel like it today, that ham you have is nowhere near as exciting as my friends!

What if I bark constantly in your face, this seems like a great fun and brilliant way to get your attention….hmm no pay out, ok I will just try harder (bark louder and for longer).

But we worked through it, we trained through it and now he is a big fluffy dufus, but one who listens and wants to work with me and loves to train and to play and just snuggle up on the settee.

It was hard work but so worth it and to this day he will still question me and still teaches me something new each and every day.

It is a humbling process, learning from your dog that life doesn't have to be so complicated, do what you get rewarded for and forget the rest!

Not a bad philosophy in my eyes!

Chapter One

Been there and got the t-shirt!

Everyone ready? Then I shall begin…Are you sitting comfortably with your dog resting quietly at your feet, dreaming of running after rabbits and oozing contentment and relaxation, this is the life, this is how it was meant to be, this is what you had always dreamed of…? Right? No?

Oh, so actually you're more like me, trying to sit down to relax but your Moo of a dog is barking for attention, chewing on anything that they shouldn't be, running round in circles causing havoc (or at least this is how it used to be for me).

My first dog was one of those extremely rare (dare I say this word?!) mongrels that came ready made out of the box so to speak. She was amazing, from day one she just fitted into our life, she was perfect (and nope this isn't rose tinted glasses looking back on times gone by) she really was perfect in every way! So easy, so trainable, so loving, so gentle she was the dog we all wish for, but are rarely lucky enough to find. However, as perfect as she was and that I can never take away from her, and she taught me so much, she did not prepare me for what was to come some 20 years later!

Ahhhh I think of the days when I just had one dog, when life was easy and it was just me and her taking on the world together and then I look down to my side and see Ezekiel, this is where my story really begins……

Story? I thought this was going to be a book about training tenacious teens that are a real Moo of a dog I hear you say, well yes it is that and we will get to that but for me to help you to understand our journey and the journey of many others like you who are at their wits end with their dog, it's good for you to understand that no one not even us 'professionals' are perfect and you are not alone!

I had wanted another dog to add to our family of three dogs for some time, I wanted a dog that could help me on my journey and be my 'stooge' dog the one that I could rely on to help me and clients and their dogs to see how life can be with a well-trained, well rounded and resilient dog. My husband was adamant we were not having another dog, but with time he came round to the fact that it was happening and if that was to happen there was only one breed for us: the ever-faithful German Shepherd.

I had grown up with shep's all my life and they are amazing dogs, loyal, clever, beautiful inside and out, but also challenging, but hey I'm a trainer that's fine and just what I am looking for. I started my search for the perfect dog and after many months of searching found my boy just up the road from me, I went to see him at four weeks of age and went every week to get to know him before he came home, building a bond ready for his introduction to the rest of our family human, dog, chicken, duck (and at the time goat and sheep).

Ezekiel came home at 8 weeks of age, he was a bundle of fluff and joy bouncing everywhere, his dog training went well, he attended classes and we were set on trying out competitive obedience (the job I had really brought him for) but it wasn't meant to be, he was amazing I was just a bag of nerves and so I decided after once in the ring we would find something else to try as neither of us were having any fun, and after all this should be fun for both of us!

You see I suffer with my nerves and anxiety and when I get worried and upset this affects my dogs (did you know dogs can hear your heartbeat, so when your heart starts to race they can pick up on this - this is where the old adage of they can feel the stress down the lead comes from).

That said, time passed and Zeke continued with his training taking and passing his Kennel Club Good Citizen Bronze test at Crufts! Wow what a dog he was, he was a superstar he was obedient, loving and everything I had hoped for (and still is)…….then it happened…….the hormones kicked in!

My wonderful relaxed, chilled out boy turned over night into a tyrannosaurus shepherd, you may not have heard of this breed before it's a mix of dog x dinosaur x well who knows but my oh my he became a challenge, he had hit his 'tenacious teens' and really was a Moo of a dog!

It was truly like someone had broken into our house overnight and swapped him out, he looked the same, smelt the same, dashed through the house at the sound of his food bowl, but suddenly he was like a crazed animal.

He couldn't relax, couldn't just lie down and sleep, he was alert to everything! If you moved he had to know what was going on, he had a real fear of missing out on everything. Even popping to the toilet had to involve him coming with me just in case something happened that he may miss out on!

He no longer knew his name, he no longer could even do simple exercises like "Sit", "Down" and "Wait". He couldn't control his excitement just going through a door, he had to dash everywhere!

Then came the barking, the jumping up, the humping, the refusing to listen to anything I asked of him.

The fun times had arrived!!!

Own up, who swapped my dog?

You don't know when or how but suddenly your lovable furball has turned into a monster (ok so maybe not a monster exactly but I bet there are times you could honestly think about rehoming them, even if you would never go through with it, it can be tempting to think about when you are deprived of sleep!)

This wasn't mentioned in the training classes, the breeder didn't mention it either? Your friends and family haven't told you about it, but here you are with terror on the end of the lead, what did you do wrong? What should you have done? Did your dog suddenly get swapped in the night for another that looks just like them?

These are all questions I have thought of myself and heard from owners of tenacious teens.

Don't worry you're not on your own and you are going to get through this (hey your parents got through you being a teen so how hard can it be right?).

Well, I would love to say don't worry they will grow out of it, or ahhhh aren't they cute look at them being all independent, but guess what, no they won't grow out of it.

The likelihood is yes, they will grow out of most of it however, they will still bring the behaviours you don't want along for the ride, unless they are shown how to behave now it's going to be a lot harder to undo these behaviours, the further down the line that you get.

Help is at hand though, and you have taken the first step to a better behaved tenacious teen by buying this book, so keep reading, follow it along and don't give up, you got this you can do it!

I believe in you and your dog to overcome this stumbling block!

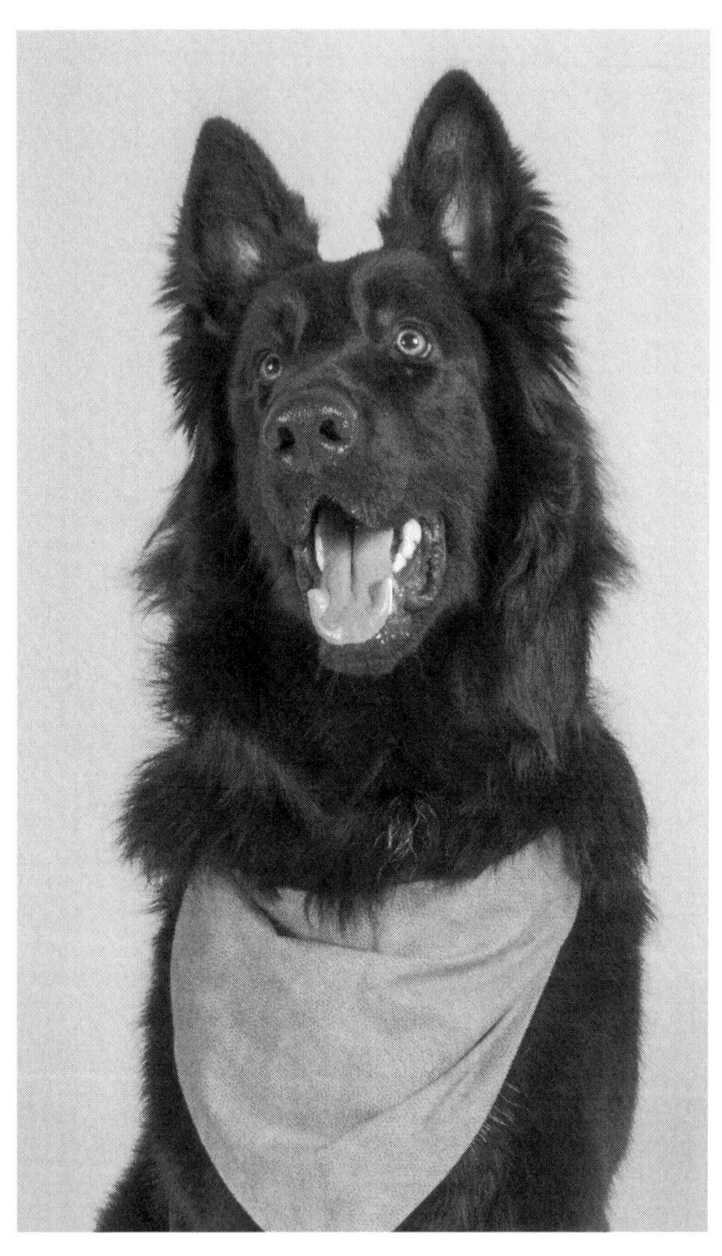

So handsome!

Chapter Two

It's going to happen!

Let's just get this bit out of the way now, you can't stop it, it's going to happen! Each and every dog goes through the teen stage, it's part of life and growing up. It's hard, it's frustrating, it makes you want to rethink the whole idea of having a dog. But trust me it is worth it (well for most of us anyway, of course there are going to be some who decide it's not for them and you know what that's fair enough, owning a dog isn't for everyone). As long as you are honest with yourself and do the best for your dog that's all that matters.

Should you get to the stage where you decide this isn't for you, I would rather the dog be signed over to a rescue centre and for them to find it the right home than for you and the dog to continue being miserable. It's a harsh reality and one no one ever wants to talk about but we need to get past that, there is no point in you and your dog being miserable for the rest of your lives together!

Of course I would much rather you get professional help so you can learn to live together but let's be clear here, what I don't want to see is a dog and human together that can't stand to be around each other and the dog ends up locked away in a crate or in the house, never going out or just left on the side of the road to fend for themselves.

The good news is if you have brought this book it is highly unlikely you are feeling that is an option, you want this to work, you want to get help and that's what I am here for!

So now we have that out of the way let's get down to it....

The teenage stage can hit from anywhere from 16 weeks of age. Welcome to the club! It's great fun isn't it! You swear the last dog you had wasn't this bad, or if it's your first dog, you swear you are the only one going through this! Well, neither is true (sorry, not sorry).

You see those rose tinted glasses you have on, take them off, reality is hitting home and hard!

This is just a stage in your dog's life, nothing more, they will get through it if you work with them and teach them what you want to see more of.

Slight side note here, those of you with the bigger breeds, mwa ha ha ha ha, you're in for a fun time!

The bigger the breed (and retrievers in general) stay in this stage for longer, German Shepherds like Ezekiel, Weimaraner's, Springers and Labradors in particular will stay in this stage until they are at least 18 months / 2 years of age (and it is highly likely you will see bits of these behaviours until they are around 4 years of age!)

It is likely you're now shouting at me through this book "but I did the puppy classes, no one warned me of this"!!!

I'm sure I trained this dog?

You did everything right, you followed the trainer's advice, you did what they said, you attended the classes, you socialised your dog in the right way, making sure they had positive experiences, you brought them up as best you could and they were let's be honest, amazing! They had the sit, down, wait, stay, leave it all figured out but since whatever has happened to them in the last few months it has all now gone out of the window!

You could swear that they have never been taught anything at all, no manners, no control, nothing, zip, nada.

It's like you have a whole new dog, that someone in the night just swapped for another that looks exactly the same but somewhere along the way had its brain removed or switched off.

Well don't panic, it's not you (well it is, kind of) but they have hit that wonderful age (which varies depending on what breed or mix of breeds and size your dog is) called adolescence!

Your dog has reached puberty and this is the time when their hormones are going haywire, they are finding their independence and strength and their brain and body are going through so many changes to be honest it's amazing they can still function as a dog at all.

Do I exist?

Selective hearing as most call it is where the dog switches off to you and concentrates on whatever has caught their attention.

I hate to tell you this but you are the problem here not the dog, not the squirrel (more commonly known as a squiggle in our house), not the prime bit of steak that someone has left out on the floor, nope it's you!

We humans are generally really boring to our dogs and let's be honest thinking back to when you were a teen did you really want to spend time with the older ones in the family, or did you want to run and play and dash and dart, and I bet you had selective hearing when it came to 'can you do the dishes'.

It's the same for our dogs, as much as they love us (and they do) we are just boring to them when it comes to fun and games, but the good news is this is one of the easiest ones to work on (nope I didn't say the easiest to fix but to work on!).

You need to get your squeak on!

Be squeaky, be exciting, change it up as often as you can, instead of a treat, have a game! Make the 3 feet around you the best place to be no matter what else is going on around you and your dog.

When playing with our dogs, why are we so sure that bouncing the toy up to and often off our dogs is the best way to get them to engage with the toy? Go on admit it, you have done this as well (I know I have) you know the one, 'get the toy' as we wave it in their face, wave it down their side and by their bum trying desperately to get their attention, bouncing it off the floor or throwing it away hoping and praying they will run after it, bring it back and we can have that time honoured game of 'fetch'!

It's hardly surprising really that many dogs see this as more of an insult than a game, we are not acting or even pretending to act or engage them in a game they know!

What we need to do is to play with them taking into account they are hunters and they like to chase prey!

Take your toy and turn it into a squirrel, dart it around a foot away from them, stop, dash around again, stop, dash back, make the toy become alive.

Often the very act of chasing the toy is more rewarding to our dogs than actually catching it, so let them catch the toy and then whip it off in another direction the moment they drop it (if your struggling with this bit use two toys, when they catch the first one, it goes dead and the second one comes alive). This type of game will really start to rev your dog up and make you more fun than what is going on around them.

A word of warning though the same as any other training you need to practice this, there is no point in going over the park where there are other dogs playing and just expecting your dog to suddenly think you are better at playing than the other dogs (sadly we can't easily compete with other dogs as we aren't a dog) what we can do is show how much more fun we can be than another dog by building this up at home first and then working in low distraction areas and building up these distractions as over time.

When you are out on your walk with your dog, put your phone away, stop thinking about work, leave your problems at home and enjoy this time with them, after all the only time they get out of the house with you is when you make that choice for them, so make it worth it!

Little steps (slowly does it)

Adolescence is a totally normal stage that all animals go through including us humans. It will pass with time but this doesn't mean you can just forget about training and start up again when they are all grown up!

This is the time to go back to basics, yep back to the exercises you learnt in puppy class (or at the very least the time to lower your expectations for a little while).

Take it slowly, don't rush them, give them time to think and to make good choices, and most importantly don't punish them for getting their choices wrong, this is the time to show them the way, and that making good choices gets rewards (really good rewards, not that left over kibble you found at the back of the cupboard).

You will get through this and this book will help you to do that, but this is a really sensitive time for your dog and they need you there to support and protect them and to show them the world is safe but also it comes with boundaries and manners.

Is my dog ill?

Just a quick side note here, when Ezekiel finally started to come out the other side of his adolescence, I regularly thought he was ill.

He would lie down and be flat out and snoring and this was something so odd to me that yep, I had him checked out at the vet (glad to say all was fine), he was just finally chilling out (at the grand age of four – German Shepherds are renowned for being really slow to mature – especially the males).

The biggest difference I noticed was all of the sudden he listened to me, yep he still had his stupid moments and I am sure he will for the rest of his life (and I wouldn't want him not to after all that's what makes him the dufus he is) but he would listen and wanted to learn and engage and to relax and to have settee time and to be loving, but this was so new to me with him (he has been by far the slowest to mature dog let alone GSD I have ever had), I really did worry he was ill.

Of course, if ever you are worried that you dog may be ill, take them to get checked out by a vet

What is a tenacious teen?

A 'teen' is an adolescent dog and like I discussed above this can occur from any time from 16 weeks of age. It can and does vary depending on the breed and size of the dog with smaller breeds maturing much earlier than larger breeds. For example, my Wire Fox Terrier was fully mature by around 12 months of age, whereas Ezekiel was nearly 2.5 by the time he fully matured physically and nearly 4 by the time his brain matured.

It's not an easy time for the dog, their hormones are swirling and they are physically changing. Whilst more noticeable in males it of course also takes place in females.

At this point their brains are also changing by deciding which neural pathways need to stay and which can be trimmed back as they are no longer used, it's not all just about the hormones (although they do play a big part) even those dogs that are neutered will still go through this stage.

Your dog has more than likely finished teething by the time they hit 8 months of age and this can have a big impact on you and them. That chew that used to take them an hour to eat, now takes moments! Those cute little nibbles on your hand now hurt (no longer needles but so much more pressure and strength behind them and could bruise you or worse could bruise or injure someone else or worse break the skin).

Suddenly your once quiet and generally asleep dog is now a raging tyrant of energy and nothing you can do will slow them down! That dog that would sleep through the night is now awake in the middle of the night whining or barking or scratching at their bed and you are losing sleep because of this and tensions are now running high.

I am afraid to tell you but this is all normal, teens generally have disruptions in their sleep patterns and will go through stages of waking up in the night and not being able to sleep and having bursts of energy but this is where training can really help (in particular brain training).

Ok so let's delve a little deeper (don't worry I won't get too 'sciency' on you).

Dog's are in many ways similar to humans, they have the same nervous system as us and pretty much the same physiology, hormones and can get scared and nervous and excited just like us.

So, think back to when you were a teen, it wasn't easy, was it. For those of you in your teens reading this book, enjoy this time it's hard but my life what I wouldn't do to have that energy again!)

It's the same for your dog, they have all this pent up energy and no way to use it up, if we don't help them to find an outlet for it they will find one themselves and this is where they become 'self employed', the problem is here is that at the same time their brain is sorting through all of their synaptic connections and deciding which ones will be of use to them in the future and which ones are redundant. If they find an 'employment' that makes them happy and feels good, the brain will keep those connections and get rid of the one that did little (that need to suckle on their mom is one of the ones that gets 'snipped' as it is no longer needed).

If your dog finds working and training fun their brain will keep that connection but if they find that chewing your shoes is way more fun and nothing can beat it that connection will also stay.

All of this is going on in your dog's brain without you even knowing it and it is all taking place at this really important development stage of being a teen. Exhausting isn't it! Hence why teens for all their energy need lots of sleep (and like us can be really grumpy if they don't get enough sleep).

I good boy?!

Motivate!

When Ezekiel was a puppy we went to a training day, the trainer asked us to come up one at a time and to motivate our dogs....great I knew this was going to go well (or rather not!)

You see, Zeke had no 'on' switch, no desire to play, no desire for food treats, no desire for much other than me to be honest with you, which was lovely but he had no desire to work. The trainer proclaimed 'well that's the first one I've seen that doesn't want anything in life! I was devastated, what had I done wrong, had I broken my dog?

Nope! Na ah! I just hadn't found what he wanted yet!

It turned out to be a specific red bone, hollow, made of horrid plastic with no squeak but he adored that bone! Problem being they stopped selling them and so the search was on again!

He is currently obsessed with a squeaky carrot (which we now have literally over 20 of to make sure he never runs out again!

It's not something I recommend, finding just one toy that your dog likes isn't going to give them, or you the variety you need to keep them engaged. That said, some dogs like Zeke are, shall we say, picky!

Hey whatever works for you and your dog is good by me as long as it isn't hurting anyone

Rocking the teen look!

Chapter Three

Play

Play is so important to my dogs. It's one of the most important things we can do to help build a bond with our dogs to use up the excess energy to keep them happy to look after their welfare. The list goes on.

Some great games to play with your dogs are hiding games like hide and seek so perhaps run in the garden and pop behind the wall then call your dog and see if they can find you. Another great game that I love to play with my dogs is tug of war.

It used to be a school of thought that playing tug-of-war with your dog would make them aggressive. However, as long as we put some rules in place and we both enjoy the game I don't have a problem with playing tug-of-war.

That said, there need to be some rules so we need to make sure that the dog gets to win often, however you need to win a little bit more often than they do!

If playing with a dog under six months of age make sure you go side to side, don't go up and down, we don't want to hurt their neck. The up and down of tug play can damage their developing bones. So make sure you are gentle in your tuggy games and if they get too excited and want to pull too hard on the toy find another game to play.

If they start to get a bit grumbly and they start to perhaps growl and get a little bit overexcited or start to nip or not realise where your fingers are then that's the time to take a break from the game and make sure they get some rest.

If your dog is getting over excited and you need to make sure you're going to win the game the easiest way to do this is to make the toy go dead. Holding onto the toy, take your hand to the ground and become really still. The dog may still try to play so it becomes really boring and the moment they take their mouth off the toy, stand up and end the game and pop them in their bed or crate with a chew to relax.

Brain games

So what can you do instead of throwing the ball or having a game of tuggy? Brain games are fantastic, otherwise known as dog enrichment games, or brain training.

Training your dog is fantastic. It wears the brain out, it tires them out and it's naturally calming to them so anything that they can lick, sniff, chew is naturally calming for your dog. Everyone that knows me knows my love of Kong toys. They are amazing! You can stuff them with their Kibble, raw food, tinned food, wet food, stuff cheese bits of ham bits of chicken turkey you name it you can stuff a Kong with it as long as it is safe for your dog it's safe to go in the Kong. The best thing to do then is to put the Kong in the freezer and leave it till the next morning when you give it to your dog it will take them even longer to finish their treat. At first they may not be quite sure what they're supposed to do with it but given time and making sure you're supervising them they will soon figure it out. There are other brands but ensure the quality of the toy can't injure them.

Another set of games that I love to play with my dogs is scent work. Getting your dog to use their nose is a great game and it's a great way to again use that extra energy that they have. I put the dog out of the room and hide treats around the house. Maybe just under the settee under a pillow a couple in their bed you name it anywhere you can think of that is safe for them to get to this is great.

When you are ready and the treats have been hidden then bring the dog back in, at first I help them to find the first one or two so it might be I lead them over to the first one, let them get the treat and instantly they are rewarded for their efforts. Then I start to encourage the dog to go and find the rest of the treats using their nose. Just 10 minutes of playing a game like this or 10 minutes of brain training is the equivalent of an hour's walk or training session. It's fantastic. I cannot recommend brain training enough.

Just be with your dog, find ways to interact with each other, what do they want to do with you? What is their favourite toy? What is their favourite game?

Ezekiel's favourite game is the floor is lava, trying to catch him as he runs past wildly waving his big fluffy tail in my face as we dash around trying to 'tag' each other.

What a clever boy!

Observe!

Ezekiel has always been, shall we say, a special dog (of course he is, they all are) but I mean in a different way, in a way only he is. He has taught me so much and I still have so much to learn from him. He is quiet and reserved whilst at the same time raging ahead to see what he is missing out on.

He gets stressed when I am stressed, he isn't keen on loud noises and mostly has no idea how to Dog!

Watching my big midnight lion (as we call him) or my fluffy butted dufus as he is otherwise known, I can get lost for hours.

If we really watch and understand our dogs they are talking to us all the time, maybe not in a language you understand yet but the good news is you can learn if you are prepared to take the time to listen!

Tractor time!

Part Two

What is my dog trying to tell me?

All chilled out!

Chapter Four

The Brain

The brain controls behaviour or rather behaviour controls the brain and so if we want to understand our dog's behaviour, we need to understand the brain and vice versa (well at least a little).

Inside your dog's brain neurons send messages back and forth to each other and this is how memories are made.

The more often a behaviour is practiced the stronger it becomes in the brain.

Imagine your dog is jumping up when greeting a person, their brain is using a ready formed path that has been practised before (imagine a well lit path in a field, we will come back to this path in a moment). That pathway in the brain is really strong so it's easier to replicate the next time they meet a person. The brain knows what to tell the dog to do - jump up!

We now want to teach the dog a new behaviour of sitting to say please, we need to build a new pathway in the dogs brain, one that says sit when you meet a new person and you will be rewarded with a treat (we need to set a new path along the field - imagine the old one is really muddy and we have our lovely new boots on!)

So, we start to use the new path but it's really dark (don't worry we have a torch to hand - your dogs treats) to help us navigate the new path. The more we use the new path (sitting to say please) the brighter the light gets for us to see where we are going. At the same time, each time we use the new path the old one gets darker (reducing the chance it will be used)

Each time we reward our dogs for sitting to say please, the stronger the new connections become in the brain (the lights get brighter on the new path - not so scary to walk the new path now is it!)

At the same time, each time we walk the new path (sit to say please) the old path gets darker (no one wants to walk along a dark muddy field!)

So setting your dogs up for success and being consistent and only ever rewarding your dog for sitting to say please when meeting someone new will soon have the new pathway in the brain lit up like Blackpool illuminations with the old pathway of jumping up dark and dank like a subway

Just don't forget that rewarding your dog when they are jumping up can also be something as simple as saying 'No', looking at them or even pushing them down

Remember what gets rewarded gets repeated, so only reward the new behaviour to light up that new path!

If you have ever heard of cognitive decline in older dogs this is where these connections and paths start to fail, the neurons can no longer fire quickly and start to die back and the dog may show signs of doggy dementia.

When your dog was born they had pretty much all of the neurons they needed, what they don't have yet is the neural connections, these don't form completely and solidify in the dogs brain until they are around 2 years of age (the bigger the breed the later this is).

It was once thought that when a brain cell or connection dies that's it but we now know that this isn't strictly true.

Brain plasticity is a process where the brain can be re-wired, so even if connections have been lost it is possible to retrain the brain to take a new pathway.

This is the same with emotional and mental experiences, the more times you do something that is rewarding (for me this is eating cake) the neural pathways get stronger and stronger, we can use this to our advantage when training our dogs.

The neural pathways that are made stronger are kept and those that are no longer used are trimmed away as part of synaptic pruning and this is why we want to make sure that the wanted behaviours get rewarded and those we would rather not see are not rewarded.

Fear

Fear is one of the few emotions that can be strong enough to create a one time learning pathway, in particular there are stages in your dog's life where they will appear more fearful than before. At around six months of age dogs go through another sensitive period (the first being at 8 weeks of age). This is where we need to be really careful with our dogs and ensure that they have the time and space to go through this period with positive experiences.

One example of this is a puppy who at six months of age hears a loud firework, it scares them and becomes such a strong pathway in the brain that they are likely to be scared of fireworks for the rest of their lives.

It may be that you don't notice this behaviour in your dog, for others it may be a clear sign that your dog is more fearful during this period, again like when they were young and learning about the world this is the time to make sure during this period they have positive experiences.

If your dog is worried during this time (usually around a week) let them explore in their own time, don't make them face their fears. Make the situation positive. At a distance they feel happy with lots of high value rewards (this doesn't just apply in these sensitive periods, this counts for all of their life!).

Helping our dogs to get through this time with positive experiences will help your dog to be a well rounded and adapted dog for the rest of their life. It may feel like hard work (because it is) but it's worth the hard work now as it will affect them for the rest of their lives.

I wish my dog could speak to me!

Have you ever watched your dog and wondered what it is they are trying to tell you? Have you ever thought I wish my dog could speak to me?

Our dogs are speaking to us, the problem is we don't understand their language or sometimes even try to (they understand ours really well!)

Teens, whether human or canine, are really good at getting our attention and annoying us but is that what it's really about? You guessed it, nope! They are trying to communicate with us!

Give me attention!!

Any parents out there will know that kids are amazing at pressing your buttons to get your attention and honestly only dogs come second to this (or so I am told, no human children here, only furry ones).

The problem is that we give our dogs attention all of the time!

Seriously, stop for a moment and don't say a word, in fact time yourself for a whole two minutes! Doesn't it feel like the longest two minutes of your life!!

This is why the stay exercise always catches people out, we never stop talking to our dogs, we are always jibber jabbering on to them, non stop.

Ok so in your two minutes that you haven't said a word (let's be honest you probably broke before two minutes) how many times did you catch your dogs attention (if they are asleep that doesn't count), did you tap your leg to get their attention, make kissy noises, make eye contact, move your position slightly did they just stare up at you with those big eyes, did you fuss them etc etc.

Yep, it's amazing isn't it, we just never shut up!

The problem being (I am the worlds worst) is when we constantly speak to our dogs they switch off from us, they like my husband, zone out of what we are saying as we are just nagging at them constantly.

You stop this attention and suddenly they are like, whoa! Why are you ignoring me! They have grown up with us always giving them attention and then we expect them to suddenly just lie down and have a sleep and not be involved in everything we do, that's a tall order for a sentient being that hangs on our every word and whose world revolves around us.

The other issue here is as you guessed it our problem again, when our dogs do something we don't like we give them even more attention! We tell them 'no', shout at them, or say 'get off the settee', 'stop jumping on me' and then often go hands on when they don't listen, pushing, pulling them into place or even just gesturing. The problem here is that all of this 'chatter' and 'hands on' is attention to our dogs and that is what they crave the most, so we are rewarding the things we don't want to see and often ignoring the ones we do want to see (it's a bit backwards really isn't it).

Remember what gets rewarded, gets repeated (we don't set what is rewarding to our dogs they do!)

Ok so this is all great but if our dogs really are speaking to us, how do I know what they are saying?

Our dogs can't speak to us in our language, but that said if you are willing to listen (or rather watch) and to learn they are speaking to us all of the time.

One of my favourite past times is people watching but even more so dog watching.

I will often just sit and watch my dogs and how they interact with each other and me and other people. Lazarus, my older boy is so clear with his signals it amazes me when I watch him. He has truly honed his skills in this area. However Ezekiel is honestly the worst, he has no clue how to 'dog'!

What I mean by this is that Lazarus can show how he is feeling to other dogs and people so easily (I will often use him to show behaviour to clients as he is so easy to watch and learn from), there is no mistaking what Lazarus is feeling and this really helps other dogs to understand when to approach and when to stay away.

A few things to note here: Black dogs are really hard for other dogs to read, in particular those that are very fluffy (like Ezekiel), other dogs can't read black dogs very well due to their faces being in shadow, on the other hand you may think that a dog that is black and white or a variation of this would be the easiest but breeds such as Huskies are also really difficult to read due to the light and shade in their faces and the markings on their fur. Dogs with big droopy ears, extreme changes to their skull or skin (such as pugs or basset hounds) are also really difficult to read when you are a dog.

We humans can however learn how to read our dogs and can help them if needed. Some of the behaviours to watch for in your dog are below, it's really fascinating to watch for these as you're out on your walk or even at home.

If we watch and listen and learn our dogs will happily tell us how they are feeling, be careful though as some of these signs are really easy to miss! Lets cover the biggest mistake most people make first - The guilty look

You know the one, eyes looking up at you with the whites of their eyes showing, ears far back on the head and generally looking sad and upset that they have done something wrong.

This is not the dog feeling guilty, this is the dog looking to appease you, they are showing submission as they would to another dog to say please, I am no threat to you please leave me alone.

So what else should I be looking for? Let's look at the more obvious signs first

Whining and whimpering

Often when a dog whines it is for attention and in many cases this is true but it's not always as simple as that, dogs will have different whimpers (like barks) to show how they are feeling, if you pay attention to your dog over the next few weeks you will be able to learn which whine they are using for different situations

Often a short whimper or whine will be to say they are excited or anxious, whereas, a long whimper could be a sign they are in pain or uncomfortable with the situation

Wide open eyes staring

If your dog starts to stare with eyes wide open (such as at another dog and especially if they hold that stare for more than a couple of seconds) they are likely showing signs that they are alert or uncomfortable and need more space, be aware though the stare could be fleeting and can be really easy to miss!

If the stare turns into an intense stare with eyes being made smaller such as narrowing of the eyes they are becoming threatening towards the other dog and telling them to stay away.

If the dog looks and then looks away they are showing that they want to be left alone but in a polite and submissive manner.

Panting

Whilst dogs will pant when they are hot to help them to cool down, they will also show this behaviour when they are stressed. If your dog is panting for no apparent reason (it's not too hot and they haven't been running around) it is likely they are stressed.

In particular if your dog is panting with a wide open mouth and a spade tongue (where the tongue expands in shape at the bottom like a spade) this is another sign they are feeling stressed.

Showing teeth

When a dog bears their teeth by wrinkling their lips up this is a warning, they are saying 'leave me alone' or I am likely to use these on you. They are stressed and do not want to be approached.

This behaviour can also be very discrete with the dog looking as if they are smiling, pulling the lips back slightly.

You often see videos of dogs 'smiling' those dogs are more often stressed.

Raised hackles

When the line of fur on your dog's back raises up this is often a sign that they are unsure of the situation around them, alert, or trying to show those around them that they are bigger and wish to be left alone.

Head tilt

Often thought of as one of the cutest behaviours our dogs show, this is a really important behaviour, tilting of the head allows the dog to establish where a sound is coming from.

Growling

Growling is your dog's way of giving a warning, a low sustained growl shows that they are unhappy with the situation, they are saying please move away and leave me alone. It is often interpreted incorrectly as aggression.

Howling

Whilst howling can be a way for wolves to communicate with each other, dogs will also use this behaviour to announce their presence to others. It can also be a sign of distress such as being left home alone. This behaviour is also commonly seen in breeds such as huskies who use it to communicate with their owners.

Exposing their belly

When a dog exposes their belly to another dog they are showing submissive behaviours to say to the other dog, I am no threat.

If you dog lies on their back with their belly exposed at home such as when in their bed they are showing they are content and do not feel threatened

Mounting or humping

A really common behaviour in teenage dogs, anywhere from around 16 weeks of age our dogs hormones will start to become more intense and this hormone level change can cause young male dogs in particular to start to show humping behaviour (also seen in females)

Your dog may also use this behaviour to elicit attention, often as it has been inadvertently rewarded, by the human encouraging them to stop this behaviour they are receiving attention and this makes the behaviour rewarding.

Bowing

The play bow (front end down with their bum in the air, often with a big wag of the tail) is an invitation to play, they are saying to the other dog (or person) let's have a game.

Walking in circles

This is often seen before the dog lies down, they are looking to find the most comfortable position. However, this can also be a sign of pain and discomfort and so it may be worth taking them to a vet for a pain check up if you see this more often than usual.

Dogs will also circle before toileting, there are many theories on this but at this time there is no solid evidence to show which of these theories are correct. Ranging from them trying to find magnetic north, to finding the perfect spot through scent.

Wagging tail

A wagging tail does not always mean a happy dog -

Happy and relaxed wag

A happy wag is usually seen through a relaxed or whole body wag where the hips may start to wag too.

Alert wag

An alert dog will stand tall with ears and tail raised, something has caught their attention.

Fast wag

The faster the tail wags the more excitement the dog is feeling.

Slow wag

A slow or barely wagging tail is often a show that your dog is insecure or unsure of a situation.

Still tail

Stopping the tail from wagging can be a sign that they are trying to appease the other party, almost a negotiation of I don't want to be a threat but please leave me alone, I'm not happy.

Upright tail

If your dogs tail stands upright and becomes still or arches over their back they are feeling threatened and trying to make themselves look bigger than they are and can help to release scent from their anal glands to mark their territory.

Straight out tail

Holding their tail out inline with their back usually shows curiosity, they have seen, heard or smelt something that has caught their attention. You are likely to see this in the pointing breeds when they also show the point (lifting on leg) that gives them their name.

Straight up in the air tail

When your dog raises his tail straight up and starts to wag it frantically they are showing that they are threatened and are not afraid to use aggression if needed.

Tail between the legs

If your dog tucks their tail under their body through the legs or for those with a tail that naturally sits high they lie it on their back they are really worried and stressed and need to be removed from the situation.

Note: A wagging dog can and will still bite or move up the ladder of aggression (as shown below), a wagging tail is not always a sign of happiness!

There are even more signals if you watch closely!

Yawning

Yawning can be a sign that your dog is stressed or facing a threat, yawning can help them to release tension. Your dog may yawn if they are confused (such as when learning a new cue). Of course your dog also yawns when they are tired, the yawning we are speaking about here is when it is unlikely they are tired. Context is key!

Licking lips

When a dog licks their lips it may be a full nose lick with the tongue going right over the nose, or it can be as discreet as a quick flick of the end of the tongue. This is one of the most missed behaviours as it can be so quick! Your dog will likely do this when they are feeling confused or worried or stressed.

Flicking ears

When your dog flicks an earole they are looking to locate the sound, it may be something that they have heard that they are not quite sure what it is or where it is coming from.

Pacing

If you dog starts to pace it could mean a number of things, from needing the toilet to being unsure about what is going on around him, if they start to run circles around you they are asking for you to play with them (but note this could also be seen as herding behaviour in some herding breeds such as German Shepherds, Collies, in which case this behaviour shouldn't be encouraged)

Sniffing the air

If your dog starts to sniff the air it may be that they have sensed there is a threat or possible prey in the area (or a bitch in heat), they are unlikely to bark or show their whereabouts.

Paw lift

A paw lift is another sign of stress, he may lift a paw and crouch as the same time making them look smaller to threat

Your dog may also touch you with their paw, in this case it is likely they are trying to get your attention.

Crouching

When a dog goes down into a crouch it is to make them look smaller and therefore less of a threat to another dog or person (this is often thought of as part of the guilty look), they are not feeling guilty they are trying to appease you.

Pricking ears

When your dog pricks their ears they are alert and if they put their ears forward this can be seen as an act of aggression towards another dog, or they may want to play. However, as it is sometimes hard to establish their emotion on this behaviour alone it is best to take it as they want more room from the other dog or person.

Flat ears

If your dog puts their ears flat against their head they are showing signs of submission and worry, they are not only protecting their ears by holding them flat to their head they are showing they are scared and want to be left alone.

Freezing

If your dog freezes even for a second or two they are feeling threatened or challenged and worried, you may see this behaviour if you pass them when they are eating, this is another way of your dog telling you they are not happy and need more room.

Leaning

Dogs which are worried, scared or stressed may lean into you, whilst this may feel like they accept you and want to be close to you (which can be the case if their other body behaviour is relaxed), this can be to help the dog protect themselves. Being closer to you and leaning on you means they can react quickly to the tiny movements of your body and limits the space you or the aggressor has to get to them

Shaking off

If your dog shakes off as if they have just had a bath but are actually dry this is their way of shaking off their adrenaline, this is one behaviour we really want to encourage and can even put on cue!

By shaking off your dog is shaking off the smell of the adrenaline so other dogs can't smell it on them as easily, it helps to relax them and so can be a really handy cue when you have walked past something that has worried them.

Ladder of aggression

When a dog reacts to something they find stressful or worrying they will follow a pattern of behaviours that can be thought of like rungs on a ladder. Developed by Kendal Shepherd and based on her experience of working with dogs.

Every rung on the ladder covers a signal or behaviour the dog may show through their body language to communicate with others dogs and us as to how they are feeling.

The more stressed or worried the dog becomes the further up the ladder the behaviour they will show.

The sooner we learn to understand these behaviours and to recognise them the sooner we can help the dog to feel more comfortable and to stop the more escalated behaviours from being seen.

The behaviours seen on the lower rungs of the ladder are the most commonly seen when a dog feels uncomfortable, going back to watching our dogs and learning their behaviours, this is a great place to start.

Keeping a diary of when you see these behaviours and the environment or action that brought on this behaviour will help you to understand how you can help your dog in the future.

It's important however, to remember that if the early signs are missed or ignored the dog will start to show the higher behaviours without first showing the lower levels.

Each time a behaviour is ignored or doesn't work for the dog they are likely to stop using that behaviour meaning you will have less warnings of their impending behaviour, the dog may in future choose to go straight to the top without prior warning!

Your dog may not show every behaviour on the ladder, they miss one or a few out, they may jump from any rung to another so it's really important to be able to recognise these and where they are on the ladder to ensure you can help them.

As you will see below the behaviours start at the bottom of the ladder with yawning, blinking and tongue flicking and build up to snap and bite.

Bite

Snap

Growl

Freeze / stare

Lying down belly exposed

Standing crouched / tail tucked under

Creeping / ears folded back

Walking away

Turning body away / sitting / paw lift

Turning head away

Yawning / blinking / tongue flick

Recognising how your dog is feeling is only part of your job in caring for your dog. To go one step further we need to understand how to help them to relax.

So now you know how to recognise your dogs behaviour and you can now communicate with your dog that little bit easier, fantastic!

Chapter Five

Stressed out Pooch! (and two legs!)

Stress bucket

Did you know it can take as little as around 20 minutes to start to calm down when stressed for a human, whereas for dogs it can take up to 72 hours! That's a really long time when you think about all that can happen in that time.

Think of it this way, your dog has a bucket with a very small hole in the bottom.

Each time something happens to cause our dogs stress they show one of the above behaviours we have discussed because they are stressed in one way or another. Each time they show one of these behaviours (whether we see it or miss it) they are adding to this bucket.

Over time this bucket lets out some stress very slowly through the tiny hole in the bottom. In the meantime stress is building up in the bucket quicker than it can empty (imagine a teaspoon a minute being let out, but a Litre a minute being put in).

Once the bucket is full they have two options (although not really options as it is affected by many things such as how we allow them to relax or events that take place around or involving our dogs).

If we allow our dogs the space and time they need by keeping them home and helping them to empty this bucket through brain training and games for the next 72 hours we can help this bucket to slowly empty on its own.

I get it, you're there thinking well I can't not walk my dog for 3 days! Well yep you can! A dog whilst they may want to go out each day can cope without a walk for a few days if needed. If you have been out on a walk where something has happened or something really stressful for your dog has taken place at home it is best to give them a few days off, where they can relax and unwind.

Think of it this way, you're at work and you get called into the boss' office, whilst it may not be anything bad this has set your adrenaline off and puts you on edge for the day. You go home and the school has called to say they need to speak to you tomorrow, before you know it your elderly parent is on the phone, they aren't well. You go to bed that night, head swimming with thoughts and you barely sleep. The next morning you get up on the wrong side of bed, with little sleep, a number of things to deal with throughout the day and let's be frank you're not in the best of moods! You know the ones, the days you just want to write off and give up and go back to bed!

It is similar for our dogs, but where we can talk to a loved one or a friend to let off steam they can't, they also have to deal with us being all stressy and this once again adds to their bucket of stress.

So your dog is stressed and we then take them out for a walk, that annoying dog down the road is also out for a walk, we spot them, our dog spots them, the other dog barks at our dog, our dog barks back and here we go again, our already stressed dog is now at the point of their bucket being at tipping point, they just can't take anymore!

The stress bucket starts to spill over the top, there is just no room left, the last straw is breaking the camel's back and our dog explodes in a fit of lunging, barking and all out craziness (it's very likely by this point the other dog is also doing this!).

The other possibility is that our dog has had a stressful few days, you have started back at work after working from home for some time, or you have just got back from a week away where their routine has changed, or the dog down the road has been out at the same time each day this week and barked at your dog, their stress levels are high!

Recognising our dogs' stress levels through watching their behaviour, we decide it is best to let them have a few days at home to relax and unwind. We play brain games with them, give them plenty to sniff, chew and lick, licki mats, filled kongs, scatter feeding all sorts and this helps them to let the water in their stress bucket slowly flow out of the tiny hole in the bottom.

After a few days you go for a quiet walk, you go out at a time when chances are the annoying dog down the road won't be out, you even get to let your dog have some time off lead and you realise your dog is already so much happier and more relaxed.

To help with your dog's stress bucket you can also make sure you help your dog when out and about using the 3 second rule, yellow dog rules and where needed preparing for muzzle training just in case you may ever need it in an emergency.

3 second rule

The 3 second rule is a really great way of making sure you pick up on your dog's behaviour, whenever they get to greet another dog or person or see something they are unsure of.

Three seconds is enough for your dog to look at the distraction, take it in and then look back at you or come away. When starting out with these exercises I usually stick to just two seconds and then build up to three. You can learn how to teach your dog this exercise later on in the book.

Yellow dog

If a dog is wearing Yellow or the person walking the dog has something yellow attached to the lead or dog (such as a yellow lead, yellow bandanna, coat or anything that says 'nervous' or such like) make sure you give them plenty of space.

If a dog is wearing yellow they need more space than other dogs, this may be due to them being unwell, recently having had an operation, not a fan of other people or dogs, or many many other reasons

The main point here is to give that dog plenty of space so you and they can enjoy their walk

NEVER allow your dog to run up to another dog that is on lead (yellow or otherwise) they are on lead for a reason (and on that note nor to a dog off lead, they don't know how they will react and it's just plain rude!).

Muzzle up project

Dogs wear muzzles for many different reasons, it doesn't always mean they are aggressive or reactive (although of course it can, and it's the responsible thing to do if they are).

Many dogs wear a muzzle as they pick up and eat items on their walks that are bad for them, from stones, to sticks, the list goes on.

Teaching your dog to tolerate and wear a muzzle is really important for all dogs, you never know when you may need one! When a dog is in pain they may react in a way that they wouldn't normally and so a muzzle is an ideal way to enable you or a vet to handle the dog without having to worry about the dog biting.

Door dashing

One way we can help our dogs is to help them to leave the house in a calm and relaxed manner, a dog that leaves the house calm will be much calmer on the walk in general. It's of course not a guarantee that you won't come across things that will cause them stress (or you) but you can help them to cope.

For those of you that don't have this problem, sit back and relax for a moment and be grateful your dog doesn't have a boundary problem (although if I am honest with you, this is unlikely and your best to follow this advice anyway, it certainly won't hurt to practice it).

I swear there were times with Ezekiel when I honestly thought I was going to be dragged off through the front door, off down the road and to Narnia, and don't even get me started on the back door!

Doors and boundaries can be huge for dogs, so first of all let's have a look at how dogs see boundaries.

The door from one room to another, oh how exciting this is (or scary!). Either something VERY exciting is about to take place in that magical other room and they just can't bear not being part of the action OR your dog is worried they are about to leave on their own and that just can't happen, the big room monster may get them!

The back door and even more so the front door, are portals to magic worlds, in these magic worlds there are sniffs galore, fox poop if you're really lucky and that magical thing the two legs call 'walkies'.

Ahhhh but don't forget there are also fences, walls, baby gates, crates, pens, the list goes on! The grass is always greener on the other side and you just have to get to it.

Then there is the front window….wait what's that there is someone coming to the window, they are getting closer!! OMG MOMMMMMMMMMMM BURGLAR, BURGLAR, BURGLAR, BURGLAR!!!!!!! Nope don't panic it's ok, I made big Woof Woof and they have gone now, job done, go me! I am the bestest dog ever, my two legs are safe!

Off we go!

`

Right we have got out of the door, past the window, past the wall and the fence here we go get ready, set and we are off…. Oooooo there is a sniff down there I MUST get to it, boiiiing hmmm there appears to be something holding me back, never mind I am a big strong boy I can do this I GOT THIS, grit your teeth and PULLLLLLLLLLL, sniff sniff, sniff '……oooo Lucy from down the road hasn't been feeling great this week her pee mail is a bit off…sniff, sniff, sniff…… hmmm….old bramble is doing well he has got his pee mail really high today at least 6 inches off the ground…… SQUIGGLE!!!!!!!!!!!!!!! MUST CHASE THE SQUIGGLE!!!!!!! I love to run and pull so surely two legs do too, I can hear shouting behind me STOP must mean she is having so much fun! I love our daily outings together. We have soooo much fun. Yank! Ahhhh two legs have pulled me back to them, they must need me to guide them over to the exciting thing, hang on I am here to help, 1, 2, 3 and off we go! Yank!, Honestly, keep up two legs! I am such a good dog, they are clearly struggling to keep up, I know, I will pull them along with me. That will help and guess what even if I can't breathe it feels sooooo good so I will just keep doing it!'

Sound familiar? I see so many people out walking their dogs (or rather the dogs taking their human for a walk) and I know it's no fun. It hurts, really hurts (both us and them)! So why do they do it?

Pulling can actually be rewarding in itself to dogs, they get to the thing they want quicker, and the tension on the neck other than potentially doing a lot of damage physically can release dopamine, most commonly known as the 'happy' hormone. So, whilst your dog is pulling you, they are actually getting a release of a hormone that makes it feel good to them and therefore there is no surprise that they continue to do it.

The Gang

Part Three

Really! Does this ever end?

Well hello there!

Chapter Six

Barking

The biggest button that my boy presses is barking! It's right up there with someone tapping me for my attention!

I was taught many years ago if you can't stop your dog from barking put it on cue, so you have an 'off' and 'on' switch, well that's great when you finally find your dog's 'off' switch but for those of us with tenacious teens it's not so easy (it's not like there is a big red button to power down the dog now is it!.....if only, or even a volume button would be nice!)

So, let's be clear here Barking is a dog's way of communicating, only when they try to do this with us humans we generally just shout and 'bark' back at them (what a great game this is!). However, as we don't speak the same language this is where the problems can start.

Think of it this way, you go to another country and go to order off the menu, you don't read the language let alone speak it, so you start to speak louder and slower to the waiting staff, they don't understand you, you don't understand them, so again you get louder and slower, this carries on until you are both so frustrated at not being able to communicate you just end up shouting (and most likely swearing at each other), this is the same situation with your dog, except your dog finds it great fun!

For example, barking at dinner time is one that really gets to me and is quite possibly one of the most common alongside barking at the postie coming to the door. The dog is most likely saying 'hey I'm hungry, hurry up will you', in a rush to stop the barking (if nothing else the neighbours are never a fan of a barking dog) we rush to make their dinner and put it down for them to eat and voila we have rewarded the barking making it more likely to happen again and again and again, after all what works gets repeated (remember this as will it become a bit of a mantra for you).

Here starts the problem (and the problem in general), we give in to our dogs all the time (yep you read that right we are the problem not the dog!).

Honestly, I don't think in all my years of owning or training dogs I have ever come across a dog that can bark as loud, or for as long as my boy Ezekiel can he is truly amazing in his skills to hit that pitch that goes right through you!

Dogs bark for a whole host of reasons, and if you listen carefully and get to know your dog's bark you can usually tell which bark is for what.

Have a listen to your dog and write down what type of barking they use for different things, it's fascinating but also a really good way to get an idea of why your dog is barking and this can then be used to look at which areas you need to work on most to help to alleviate the barking.

Your dog isn't barking to annoy you, they are doing it because they don't know what else to do (although it can feel that way!) and it's great fun when two legs join in!

There are five main types of barking that can be easily recognised once you start to listen to your dog

Fear barking

Warning barking

Frustration

Excitement barking

Learned barking

Note: frustration and excitement can be easily confused with each other but they are different

Fear barking

This bark tends to be high pitched and in a series of longer barks, this is generally seen as a call for help. The dog is likely to be full of adrenaline they may run back and forth as if trying to get out of confinement, if they are on the lead it may become more aggressive sounding as they are trying to tell the scary thing to stay away, it's not aggression per se they are trying to say 'leave me alone' and most likely their other warning signals have been ignored (more on this in a little while).

The most important notes here are that your dog is scared or worried, do not reprimand them, do not make them face their fears, reassure them, show them that you will protect them and you will take them away from the scary thing and keep them safe.

Fear barking is a very emotional bark for the dog, they are hyped up on stress hormones and they may feel you're not listening to them and neither is the thing that is scaring them. Try to remember this and when your dog does bark through fear try to empathise with how you would feel if you were on the end of a lead and unable to get away from what scares you most, this will help you to stay calm, after all your dog will pick up on your emotions as well.

Warning barking

This is a really easy bark to recognise. This is the bark your dog uses to warn you something is coming that they don't feel is safe. You may not hear it as often as you think but it's the one that for me personally always gets my attention.

It's a short sharp 'woof' usually heard from my older lad Lazarus when the neighbour's cat is in the garden. Whilst the rest are excited and frustrated as they can never actually get close to the cat as it sits on top of the fence just peering at them, Lazarus sees it as an assault on the household!

The problem here is that Ezekiel has learnt this behaviour from Lazarus (we will go over learned barking below), so now I have a cacophony of excited, frustrated and warning barks all in one go (or at least I did).

Frustration barking

Ahhhh the frustration bark, Ezekiel's favourite bark followed closely by the excitement bark, this one is aptly named as it frustrates the hell out of me and usually means that Ezekiel is frustrated at not being 'involved' in all the action that is me sitting down to drink a cuppa and relax for those precious five minutes before I carry on again.

You know the one, the one where you're just settling down, your comfy, your cuppa is at the perfect temperature to drink and then there it is……

That never-ending series of 'woofs' possibly with a howl at the end, before it repeats itself like a broken record. Your instincts tell you to shout, yell, plead, beg, anything to just get them to stop barking! But to no avail, as you will learn later and above, answering them is just going to make this the best fun ever.

It is important to remember though that your dog is barking as they are frustrated, more than likely as they have been left somewhere and they cannot cope on their own. The biggest time for this is when you leave the house, or put them in another room.

Excitement barking

I'm pretty sure you will know this one really well, the high-pitched hysterical bark when you come home through the door. The 'you have been away for ever and ever and ever' (ok so like 10 minutes but hey that can feel like forever to your dog).

Usually seen with a wiggly butt, waggy tail, and lots of movement due to the dog's heightened levels of adrenaline that is now pumping round their body it is near on impossible for them to be still, they literally can't control themselves, it's like a pressure cooker waiting to implode the excitement is palpable.

If they really can't control themselves their mouths may come into play, mouthing, jumping, up, spinning on the spot, the lot (not so fun when they are no longer that cute tiny little dog though is it!).

Learned barking

This is a great one to look out for, and is fascinating to watch. Lazarus will bark once, a huge big 'woof' and then stop and look around to see who is going to react (usually Ezekiel), this is the bark your dog learns to do as they have somehow been rewarded for it (usually with the owner having no clue they have inadvertently been rewarding it).

Going back to Lazarus for a moment he is the King of the learned bark. From an early age he learnt that if he gives out one huge 'Woof' all the others will jump off the settee and run to the window to see what is going on, mom follows suit to check for any 'burglars' – nope no burglars here 'not a sausage to be seen' - other than Ignatius that is.

In the meantime Lazarus has looked around and seen that everyone is now engaged in the big burglar search and is now legs akimbo on the settee all to himself, result! This he learnt from our little Wire Fox Terrier when he was just a pup.

Ezekiel learnt this behaviour too but put his own little spin on it, one big 'woof' and mom pays attention to you. Suddenly you have the human's total attention and what's even better is if you carry on, they come over to see what is going on. There you have it, a woof and a reward and what gets rewarded gets repeated.

Stop barking!

There are a number of things you can do to help your dog to understand that barking isn't going to be rewarded. Of course using training to teach them an alternative behaviour is best but if you don't have time for that right now then management can also be used in the short term.

By managing your dog in the short term whilst you look for someone to help you to train your dog around their barking this can take the pressure off you a little (and hopefully show your neighbours you're doing all you can to keep things quieter).

Let's start with a dog that is barking when they leave the house whether this is fear, excitement or frustration barking, we need to help the dog to feel calmer about the situation.

The biggest reason I get called out for barking is fear of, excitement at the sight of or frustration that they can't get to other dogs.

Imagine this, you are out on a walk and suddenly another dog comes into sight, before you know it your dog is barking (and quite possibly lunging) reacting to the dog they can see.

The problem here is that as owners we start to anticipate this behaviour before we have even left the house! We set off on our walk thinking 'please don't let us see another dog', 'what if we see another dog', 'I have a big dog, what if I can't hold them', 'my little dog is so embarrassing when he barks at the big dogs' and so on……

I get it, I really do! I have been there! It's also really hard as you want your dog to enjoy their walk and you want to enjoy it with them but you know the moment you step out the door, all bets are off and you can't wait to get round your walk and get back home to safety!

In the first place you can manage this situation the best you can. Taking your dog out early in the morning, or later on at night when there aren't so many dogs around will help you and your dog to start to feel more comfortable. This may feel like a great inconvenience but it really is the first step in helping you both to relax.

When you go out of the house stressed and worried you are putting your dog on the back paw straight away. If two legs are worried then I really have something to be worried about!

If when you are out you see another dog, turn around and give your dog more space. This may very well mean walking all the way back the way you came or even turning around a few times to get away from the other dog. Your dog needs more room!

You may also have a dog that lunges towards the distraction.

Lunging

Lunging especially on the end of the lead when out on a walk is usually but not always a sign that the dog is over aroused. They have either seen something that they are so excited about and they just can't control themselves as it's just too amazing, or they have seen something that has scared or worried them and they are trying to tell the scary thing to stay away in the only way they know how (see the escalation of dog behaviour).

Whether your dog is over aroused due to excitement we need to show your dog that the more excited they get the further away the exciting thing gets, calm and controlled gets you access (not to everything but to the things the human feels is safe we're not about to allow them to go get access to that squirrel).

Side note: Lunging can occasionally be brought on by pain so if your dog has suddenly started lunging it is always best to get a full check up with your vet.

To help your dog to relax in situations where they may feel lunging is the best way to react (refer to the ladder of aggression and you will see it is quite possible if we don't eat with this now the behaviour will escalate), we need to help them to feel calm and confident.

The best way to deal with this issue is to get professional help from a dog trainer or behaviourist. Speak to a professional who can come in and help you to work with your dog and show you exercises and tips on how to help your dog feel more comfortable around other dogs.

You can make a really good start on helping your dog by looking at the below training exercises that you will find in the second half of this book, but not just yet!

- Door control - leaving the house in a calm way will help you and your dog to be calmer on a walk

- Distractions and ideal learning distances - we want to set our dogs up for success so learn how to ensure your dog is in place where they can learn the right way

- Watch me - this will help your dog to keep their attention on you, rather than the scary/exciting dog/person/item/situation before them, make sure they have plenty of room from the thing that is making them feel this way so that they feel comfortable to keep their attention on you (set them up for success)

- Look, look back - here we are going to teach the dog that they can look at the thing that is making them feel emotional but they then look back at you for reassurance (building in the 'Watch me' for longer attention on you)

Boundary barking

Let's now look at what to do if your dog barks when someone comes to the house.

We need to help our dogs to understand that yes this is, let's be honest here, their job! No point in having a dog and barking yourself (but guess what that's what we do all the time!)

Imagine the situation (I am pretty sure we can all relate to this one). The postie turns up at the door, your dog relaxed and enjoying a snooze suddenly wakes up, runs towards the door or window and yells as loud as they can 'Danger!! Danger!! Someone is approaching the house, this is NOT a drill!!! Danger!!!

We end up shouting 'shut up', 'enough', 'thank you!', 'come away' (it could be your shouting Rhubarb it doesn't matter what you are saying you are barking WITH your dog!)

Your dog at this point is thinking wow this is AMAZING! I woof, two legs join in, I am such a good dog!

Then the best part happens, the postie, as they have a habit of doing, comes towards the door, breaches the defences and pushes the letters through the threshold to the family home that must be protected at all costs!

Dog barks like crazy, you bark like crazy and Postie goes away! Job done! Best dog ever!!! We did it, we worked together and we protected the house from utter destruction by a few letters! Wow I am the best dog ever, I have the best two legs ever, what a team we make!!!

You may be inwardly laughing here thinking, errrr, yep that sounds about right but it's true this is what is occurring!

So how do we stop the barking?

Time, patience and a lot of both to boot!

There are a number of things we can do here to help to start to manage the situation, the easiest is to stop your dog from accessing the door and window where people approach the house.

Close the curtains, blank out the windows, put the dog in another room, these will all help in the short term. Longer term, putting an external post box at the end of your drive can really help, so the postie doesn't have to come as close to the house.

However, let's be honest it's not realistic to keep your dog away from the front door and windows all of the time long term so we need to start to associate the door and window with a reward coming from another place that's even better!

This is where you need your extra yummy treats!

Have a few pots of treats around the house so you always have treats to hand when you need them.

You will at the very least need one by the door and one by the window and one in the next adjoining room at least.

A few friends can really help here, and if your postie is as amazing as mine they may even be willing to help a little each day.

We need to teach our dogs that when someone approaches the house their reward will come from the room away from the door or window. You see barking in itself is rewarding to your dog, so not only are they being rewarded as they are succeeding in making the 'burglar' go away each time they come to the house, just the sound of their own voice is rewarding along with the wonderful cocktails of neurotransmitters that are released in their brain.

So yep you guessed it, we need the rewards to be even better!

Start off with a friend walking past the house, where your dog barely notices (we do need your dog to notice or they aren't going to learn anything) but don't want your dog to react with barking. As soon as the person starts to pass the house, get your dog's attention with a tasty treat and throw it away from the door or window that they are paying attention to. They are being rewarded for moving away and staying calm.

Now practice this with the person at the same distance from the window or door until the dog automatically looks for their treat - person starts to walk past the end of the drive, dog takes this as their cue their reward is coming and looks behind them, they get their reward.

Once they can do this three times in a row on three separate occasions (with at least 30 minutes in between each session) you can move on to the next step.

Ask the person to walk as if they are going to come up your drive towards the house, just one step and then retreat. Follow the steps above with your dog and yep you guessed it, once they can come away automatically for their treat three times in a row on three separate occasions you can increase how far the person comes towards the door or window.

Chapter Seven

Too quick, too close!

Don't rush this, like with any training we need to give our dogs time to work this through and to feel confident in what they are supposed to be doing.

Remember they have practised the old behaviour of barking for a long time! So we need to re-write the path in their brain so the old one fades away.

If you go too fast, each time they bark they are self rewarding the old behaviour and making the old path light up.

Slow and steady, set your dog up for success! If they are struggling with people even walking past your house at the end of the drive, or they suddenly can't cope again, go back a step or two to where they are comfortable and are able to let the person go past the house without them reacting by barking and are once again looking for their treat in the opposite direction. Do this for a few more sessions before moving on again.

There will be blips, there will be times where no matter how hard you have tried someone comes up to the door or window and the dog reacts with barking. Do NOT bark with them, encourage your dog out of the room with a tasty treat, before you answer the door.

The person on the other side will understand if you explain when the dog is away that you are working on helping your dog to understand they don't need to bark every time someone comes to the house, if the visitor doesn't understand this then quite frankly that is their problem not yours!

People coming into the house

Jumping up

Quite possibly one of the most annoying and aggravating behaviours your dog can have in my personal opinion.

From a legal point of view just to give you an idea of why jumping up can be so disastrous, a dog that jumps up could be seen as a dangerous dog. Yep, I know you think that's crazy but it's true!

For a dog to be seen or reported as a dangerous dog it doesn't have to cause any harm to a person physically, just the thought by another person that the dog could potentially harm them is enough, if a person 'fears' that the dog may harm them they can report it as a dangerous dog incident, harsh but true.

To be honest dogs jumping up is one of my biggest pet hates, now don't get me wrong if you like a dog that jumps up that's totally up to you, but my advice would be to put it on cue so that you tell the dog when to jump up, they don't just do it randomly to the person walking past or coming to your door.

Tenacious teens are particularly tenacious when it comes to jumping up and this is usually down to the owner not knowing how to stop it with them and others inadvertently rewarding the behaviour along with the dog 'just wanting to say hello' and random passers-by just wanting to fuss the nice doggy.

Stop jumping up!

So you have a rambunctious teen that loves to jump up and greet people, but how do we stop this?

Start with someone you know (or yourself if they jump up at you as well).

Each time the dog jumps up you are going to do your very best to ignore them (easier said than done I know), don't look at them, don't make eye contact, don't tell them 'no', don't speak to them, don't push them down don't do anything at all. Just ignore them!

When they finally put all four paws on the ground, reward them with a treat and fuss. If they start to jump up again, stand up straight and ignore them.

We need to let the dog learn for themselves that the only time they will get a reward is when all four feet are on the ground.

If you are finding this really difficult you can throw treats to the floor as the dog approaches you so they are then busy sniffing the floor when they get their reward of a treat from the floor.

Side note here, we don't want the dogs to learn that they snuffle up all the treats and then jump up. If they do this, move back and ignore them until they have all four feet on the floor and then try again.

Another thing to be aware of is dogs that offer four feet on the floor and then jump up, here they learn a routine of jump up, four feet on floor, reward, jump up, four feet on floor, reward, jump up and the cycle goes on and on.

If the dog jumps up after having a reward for all four feet on the ground, we need to start to extend the time they have all four feet on the floor for.

If this is the case, try this, the dog jumps up, they are ignored, four feet on the floor, count to three, if the dog is still on the floor they get a reward, if they jump up after this, they don't get a reward when their feet are back on the floor.

Move away a step or two and approach the dog again, this time they only get a reward if they remain with all four feet on the floor, any jumping up means we reset by taking a step away and approaching again.

Soon they will realise for themselves that the only way to get a reward is to greet you with all four feet on the floor.

Now comes the really hard bit! Other people!

Each time you meet someone and your dog wants to jump up you need to either

1. move away so your dog can't get access to the other person to jump up

or

b) Tell the other person to stay away until your dog has all four feet on the floor

Explaining that your dog is in training is usually enough for other people to understand, explain that when they approach if the dog goes to jump up they are to move away and they are only to reward the dog when all four feet are on the floor (don't forget this includes even looking at the dog or telling them no).

The main point here to remember is NOT to speak to, look at, put your hands on them to push them down or away, IGNORE them!

If you need to do something to stop them from jumping up and holding on to you with their paws walk into them, not away from them, this makes this position slightly less stable for them, but make sure you do this without speaking to the dog, we don't want this to be on cue, we want this to be an automatic response when greeting someone.

Eventually when you have this in place and your dog can keep all four feet on the floor every time they meet someone knew you can build in the 'sit to say please', here we are asking the dog to sit to say please for whatever they want, be that to greet someone knew, a treat or chew, or even their dinner, this then becomes their default position (check out chapter thirteen).

A great way to practice your new skills for a dog that jumps up and to build confidence in asking people to not fuss your dog until their four feet are on the floor is to practice this with a friend whilst your dog is on lead.

Mouthing

Do you remember those days when your cute little dog would chew on your hands and those little teeth like razors would leave you covered in scratches; those were the days! If you have a dog that is continuing to do this you're probably not having much fun!

More than it not being any fun, you really don't want your dog mouthing at you or anyone else, its painful and some dogs don't know their own strength (generally when dogs play they automatically inhibit the amount of pressure they use – they are taught this from a very young age by their mom, and all the play fighting with their siblings really helps here). To be honest though no matter how much they inhibit their bite or mouthing it hurts, simple!

Some will do it to get to the treats, some just want to get your attention (that sort of nagging poking you used to do to your parents) I honestly see it as them going 'Oi' 'oi' 'Oi' 'oi' it drives me nuts, it's rude and honestly I just want to scream at the top of my voice 'WHAT DO YOU WANT!!!!' but it's not like they can answer me, and shouting isn't going to get you anywhere (honestly it may make you feel better for a moment but it will only make the situation worse and turn it into a great fun game!).

Shouting at a dog for mouthing or pretending to be hurt by the dog as if you're a dog and saying 'ow' isn't going to work either, if anything it may distract them for a moment as it's a novel noise but that's about it.

Teething is a natural for a dog, like a child they explore their world through their mouth so it's our job to make sure that they are they able to carry out this natural behaviour in a way that is acceptable to us and them and guess what, if we don't work on this when they are cute little dogs, it carries on into their teens and adult life, only now it can really get them into trouble!

Kong toys are great for this and even better when filled with some yummy treats and live yoghurt or squeezy cheese, fill the Kong up and then pop it in the freezer when it's ready, give it to your dog in a quiet place where they can relax and chew on the Kong. Because it is frozen it will take them longer to get at the treats and it will encourage them to lick at the yummy filling. (There are other brands but ensure they are safe)

Chewing and biting is also a naturally calming behaviour to your dog so giving them an outlet for this is really beneficial to all, they have acceptable toys to chew on instead of your prized belongings and also it takes the attention away from your hands and arms.

Nipping can also be a sign of over arousal or your dog being overtired.

Over arousal

When playing with your dog if they start to nip at you it is likely their adrenalin levels are going up, at this point they are becoming over aroused and excited. When playing with your dog, if they nip you, stop playing for a moment and ignore them. When they stop nipping, reward them with a treat or gently play again making sure play is calmer.

It's really cute when they lunge and stalk your hands going along the floor but this will make your hand look like a toy to the dog. Whilst we want the dog to be used to being handled all over, using our hands to play with the dog instead of using a toy can encourage them to nip, it's much better to use your hands to hold a toy they can play with.

If you're playing with a toy and your dog starts to nip, slow play down, if that doesn't work stop play and sit still, as soon as they stop nipping offer them a reward of a treat or your attention again. If you do start to play again, keep it calm and relaxed, again as soon as they nip, play stops.

Another way to teach your dogs that your hands are not for nipping is to hold a treat in your hand and fold you fingers around it so it's in your closed fist, offer the your hand to the dog they may start to sniff and nuzzle at your hand, wait for them to stop, as soon as they do offer them the treat.

Overtired

Tired dog can mean bitey dog. Teen dogs in particular need a lot of sleep, anywhere from between 16 to 18 hours a day, and just like human children if they are over tired, they can become grumpy

If you are playing with your dog or have been training with them, they are going to use the only way they know how to try to tell you they are tired, nipping.

A tired dog may nip at you and this may increase in determination when they are tired, they are trying to say I am tired now, I need a sleep (think of a baby crying this is their only way of telling you they are tired, it's the same with your dog).

If your dog is now biting and nipping at you there is a good chance they need a sleep, pop them into their quiet area and give them a Kong toy or other suitable toy to chew on and let them relax and sleep. If you have children this is the time to explain to them that the dog is tired and they need their sleep and so they are not to be disturbed.

Ideally, we want somewhere in the house that is just for the dog, so a crate or bed in the kitchen with a baby gate on the door can work really well so the dog isn't disturbed

Nipping of legs

If you are finding that your dog is nipping at your legs as you walk past it's a great idea to have a toy in your back pocket or really close to hand, as soon as they start to nip on you, give them the toy to play with instead of your legs

We want to teach our dog that whilst it is great fun to play together, we can also play on our own (we may want to settle down and watch the television, or eat dinner) this is the time they learn how to play on their own.

Although these toys need to be used under supervision (as do all toys and treats) they are great for alone time play:

Snuffle mats are a great toy for dogs to use on their own and are calming in nature, the dog snuffles through the long pieces of fabric in the toy to find the treats you have put in for them. Sniffing is a naturally calming and rewarding behaviour and so a great one for the dog to do on their own and one that shouldn't cause them to become over aroused (snuffle mats are available from most online pet stores, ebay or amazon and come in many different sizes and colour combinations).

Licki mats are another great alone time toy, you spread some of their dinner or liver paste or squeezy cheese on the mat and the little rivets on the mat make it harder for them to get it off, they really have to lick and lick to get to the goodies (popping it in the freezer first makes it even longer lasting), these are usually just a few pounds to buy and are great for settling your dog down in their bed whilst you relax in the same room

Of course filled frozen kongs are great too!

Woof! By Olivia Bassett

Part Four

Ok enough now, I'm tired! Help!!!

Windows to the soul

Chapter Eight

Sleepy time

One of if not the biggest reason I get called out to problem behaviours in teen dogs is caused by lack of sleep!

As discussed above teens need around 16 hours of sleep a day, which is a hell of a lot of sleep when you think about it! Now take into account that dogs have a 20 minute sleep cycle and it's easy to understand that most teens do not get enough sleep.

Now add in the raging hormones, the busy household, the fear of missing out on something amazing happening and before you know it your dog is getting very little sleep, and probably even less of the kind of sleep they need to recuperate.

We all know that really our dogs shouldn't be sleeping in our beds with us but so many do, and you know what, if that works for you that's fine, but is it really working for you?

A dog that sleeps on the bed can cause a whole host of issues and behaviour challenges that you may not have associated with sleeping on your bed with.

Separation anxiety related behaviours, over tired or over aroused, fear of missing out, cranky and nippy can all be associated in part to sleeping on your bed. Not to mention when they grow up and are suddenly taking up the whole bed you struggle to move in bed, or they decide they don't want to let anyone else share the bed with you.

Ideally for you and your dog they should have their own sleeping area, preferably in a low traffic area of the house, for my dogs this is the kitchen. If they need or want to get away from it all they take themselves off to the kitchen for a snooze (we have a big 'L shaped kitchen and our dogs will generally go and lie by the back door down at the other end of the kitchen where they know they will rarely be disturbed, especially over night. From when they were pups they had their crate set up here and this has become their 'safe place'. They settle here and are relaxed in this place).

You may decide you prefer to have a crate set up permanently for your dog and that is fine and honestly something I recommend (door left open as they get older so they can choose when to go in and out) or you can eventually replace this with a bed in the same place, somewhere they feel comfortable and safe to go to where they won't be disturbed.

Think of it this way, when they were puppies and you had to get up every few hours or even every few minutes to let them out to the toilet, you were exhausted! Very likely you were cranky and not really a pleasure to be around. You go through the day hyped up on caffeine and probably had bursts of energy when you felt you could take on the world right before you crashed out. When you went to bed you were so overtired that you would wake up at the slightest movement of your pup (after all what were they about to get up to?!).

It's very similar for our dogs, they need good quality sleep to be able to function properly.

Just because your teen is racing around the house doing zoomies doesn't mean they aren't tired, they are likely overtired and need a time out! I don't mean time on the naughty step, but more a time to relax and sleep.

If your dog is nipping, or being a 'fool' they are trying to tell you in the only way they know how they need a rest (it may not appear that way and they may protest at first but soon they will be asleep if given the right opportunity to sleep).

So make sure to offer your dog something to chew, lick or sniff as this is naturally calming for them and will help them to relax, do this in their bed or crate and you will be setting them up for success. Pop them in their crate or bed with their chew and leave them to it (of course keeping an eye from a distance that they are safe with their chew), BUT do not keep going over to check on them! Each time you go over to them you are arousing their interest again and breaking the cycle of relaxing on their own.

If you do need to go past them it's best if they are in a crate so they are safely confined, walk past without looking at them, remember even eye contact is rewarding to your dog. At first they may kick up a fuss but ignore them and leave them to settle again with their chew and before you know it they will be asleep or at least resting.

Side note: this isn't a one time deal! They need to learn through positive repetition that when they go in their crate it's time to rest, they aren't missing out, they aren't going to suddenly combust (although some may believe they are - this is where crate training will come in) they need to sleep or at the very least relax, this is their safe place.

Some dogs will need help to understand what a crate is for but most reputable breeders will have used a crate in one fashion or another from the time of the dogs birth, be that a whelping pen and then a puppy play pen to individual time getting used to a crate.

A crate really is worth its weight in gold, need to pop out for a couple of hours and want your dog to relax, pop them in their crate, staying away overnight with your dog - a crate can help to not only keep them safe but make them feel safe, it is their little den of comfort and safety.

Crate training

We can't however, just expect our dogs to come ready made with an acceptance and understanding of what a crate is for! We need to help them to understand it is their safe place and a nice place to be.

Start out by having the crate set up in the place you want it to be eventually, this will help your dog to become accustomed to it being there with no pressure on them to go in just yet. If this is possibly the first time they have seen a crate leave it there, open it with a nice bed in for a few days before moving onto the next stage.

Once your dog is used to the crate and they have perhaps even popped in to investigate on their own we can start to associate the crate with having a nice relaxing time.

Next time you feed your dog, feed them in the crate, leave the door open so they don't feel confined, we want them to know for now they can come and go as they feel they need to.

Once your dog is happy with eating out of the crate with the door open you can start to shut the door whilst they are eating, if at any point they become distressed, re-open the door and leave them to eat, we need to make sure every experience of the crate is a positive one.

The main point here is slowly, slowly does it, we want the crate to be a place where they are comfortable, relaxed and a place they freely go to when they want to sleep in a safe place.

If your dog is happy eating in there with the door shut you can start to give them a time out in the crate with a chew with the door shut, leaving them to enjoy their chew and fall asleep throughout the day for short periods.

If you dog however, starts to whine or bark when they are in their crate, try not to react unless they are in a state of panic, if this is the case you have gone too fast and need to go back a few steps and start again, be aware the faster you go the more chance you have of spoiling the crate for them so slowly does it is best!

If your dog wakes up and becomes bored in their crate and starts to whine and bark for attention try to ignore them and wait until they have been quiet for two whole minutes before letting them out, we want to make sure they don't learn to bark and whine to get attention and to be let out.

Ideally you want to make sure your teen gets at least three sessions during the day in their crate to relax and sleep for at least 30 minutes at a time, and even better if they choose to go in there themselves for a rest, that is what we are aiming for!

So next time your dog starts to nip or gets over excited or overtired, pop them in their crate with a chew and leave them to rest, you may be surprised by how long they sleep.

A quick side note:

If your dogs crate is in a room where you will need to pass it, ignore them as you do, if they wake up to look what is going on or get excited as you have entered the room, ignore them and they will soon realise there is no point in waking up and will continue to sleep whilst you get on with your day.

This time on their own is so important, they need time out the same as we do and it will also help to associate time away from you as being a good thing, such as when you need to pop out to do some shopping!

Exercise

Exercise for your tenacious teen is really important but it needs to be planned carefully, this is particularly important with the larger breeds as they take longer to finish growing and maturing.

At the same time their brain needs exercising and this is where a job comes in handy, I don't mean that you have to have a specific job for your dog such as a search dog, agility dog or competition obedience dog (unless you want to that is) I mean that they need to work their brain through training.

We all know dogs need to be walked, there is no disputing that but at the same time the type of walk is also important, especially for your tenacious teen.

How much exercise?

This is a really good question and one I hear all of the time. There are so many differing thoughts on this and I would always recommend you speak to your vet in the first place if your dog has any injuries or medical conditions. But let's keep it simple. Ideally your dog should be going for walks that are no longer than five minutes per month of their life so if you have a six-month dog you should be looking to have a maximum of half an hours walk a day.

There are many that will cite a dog will stop when it's tired well let me tell you differently, Lazarus did he was very good if he was tired he would just lie down and go 'I've had enough now', however, Ezekiel was a different story altogether and still is. Ezekiel is and always will be my most challenging dog I have ever had but at the same time I've learnt so much from him.

When Zeke was about 16 weeks of age I remember taking him to the park with some friends and their dogs, everybody else was racing round and he slipped and he hurt himself and that still didn't stop him I still had to chase him down and pick him up and we had to pop off to the vets, thankfully all was fine. When I spoke to the vet she said that he would stop when he's tired and I explained but he really doesn't he will keep going and going and going.

Private dog fields

The best reward you can give your dog is time off lead, that said especially with teens it can be really hard when there are so many people with dogs over the local park and theirs and yours really want to get to each other and you have no idea if they will get on!

You know how it goes, you get over the park and there are a number of dogs playing beautifully and you look on longingly thinking I would love my dog to be able to go over there and play and frolic but stop right there! This isn't the best way for your dog to be rewarded (especially not with dogs that are an unknown) it may be that another dog that isn't so friendly comes bounding over and your dog still on lead (or off lead) isn't so sure how to react, before you know it your arms are twice their length, the leads are tangled, or your dog is chasing another around the park or vice versa, its mayhem!

Now I'm not saying don't ever walk your dog in a public park or where there are other dogs but especially with a teen it can be a great idea to use a private dog field, you can rent private dog fields all around the country and these are ideal for working on your recall with no distractions and to help teach your dog that they really don't need to be off playing with other dogs, you are the best thing since sliced bread and you and they can have so much more fun together!

Remember this as well, when you get to the field or park (wherever you're going to be letting them off for a run, keep them on lead for a few minutes first.

We all do it, we walk or drive the same way to the off lead area, get out of the car and just let the dog go (if safe to do so) or we walk to where it's safe and then let them straight off. Before you know it your dog is a wound up ball of springy stuff, pulling on the lead, screaming and running rings around you! It's the very least you can do to let them straight off lead to give your arms a break!

The problem here is this teaches the dog this is what they are supposed to do!

Yep you guessed it again, you're the problem here not the dog!

If using a private field when you get to where it's safe to let them off:

- Keep them on lead and walk around for a little while

- Wait until they are calm, then pop the lead off and let them be!

- Let them sniff, have a run around, don't keep calling them back every five seconds, let them be a dog!

- When you do call them back:

Make sure to vary what you do when they come back to you but **ALWAYS** reward them with a fuss, a treat or a game!

- Occasionally call them back, give them a treat or reward and then let them go again
- Then next time pop their lead on for a few minutes, walk around and then let them off again.

The worst thing we do as dog owners is to pop the lead on at the end of every walk, that being the only time we call them back to us. When we do this we signal to the dog and teach them that the only time we call them back is to have their lead on and go home, play ends, end of fun off home we go.

Of course the problem here is then you have a dog that won't want to come back or when they do they start to jump around and make it a game, we get frustrated, the dog gets frustrated and we all end up going home exhausted and cranky from what should have been a great time out.

Ball chasing!

Chasing balls is great fun for dogs there is no doubt about it but do we actually know the damage it can do to them?

If there is one thing I would ask you to do it is to not allow your dog to keep chasing the ball over and over and over again especially when they're really young.

Young dogs up to the point of where they mature (which for larger dogs can be anything up to 2 years of age) have bones that aren't quite connected yet. They are growing and their bones are gradually hardening up. By keeping chasing after a ball it can cause damage to their bones and their muscles.

It may seem like great fun, you throw the ball the dog runs and gets it, they bring it back to you and you throw it again.

It's a great and easy way to exercise your dog without having to really do too much yourself.

However, the sharp turns and constantly running out and then turning and spinning and running back isn't really any good for our dogs.

On top of this all we are doing by exercising our dogs in this way is building an athlete. The more they run, the more they need to run, and, want to run. The more we build up their energy and the more we build up their stamina the more we need to be out there doing this again and again and again.

Chances are when you get home your dog is still ready to go out and have another three walks!

Chapter Nine

Neutering and adolescence

This may come across as a little controversial and it is for each person to make their own decision after consulting with an expert such as your vet, but one thing that can affect how your dog behaves is being neutered early. I am all for stopping unwanted litters of dogs and I know the risks of keeping a dog entirely, but I will never again personally have a dog neutered early unless there is an absolute medical need.

Ezekiel was neutered at 3.5 years of age, some say this may be the reason he was slow to mature, however in my personal experience leaving his dangly bits on for longer helped him to mature, furthermore studies have now shown that especially in male large breed dogs it is more beneficial to leave the dog entire until they have finished growing, allowing the testosterone to tell their body to stop growing.

Ezekiel was quite a nervous lad to be honest and continues to be a bit noise sensitive, this was another reason for leaving him entire for so long, testosterone is a confidence building hormone and so by taking that away there was a fear that it could make him more fearful, and so I worked on building his confidence through training before having that taken away.

Many will say neutering calms a dog, however this is very much dependent on the dog in general it's really a 50/50 chance and for me the benefits of waiting outweighed the risks but please make sure you speak to your vet (even two or three if you can to get an good all round view) and do your research as once they are off they can't be glued back on. There are also other options available – Ezekiel had an implant that stopped him from producing testosterone for six months before he went to be neutered so we could see how it would affect his behaviour before the big chop! I can honestly say it was the best thing for us and Ezekiel and after six months we did decide to have them removed, but I have known a number of people who having gone down the Implant route, have decided not to neuter when they have seen how the lack of hormones has affected their dog.

Dinner time!

Feeding

Feeding your dog seems really simple doesn't it! You put some food in a bowl and pop it on the floor and presto one dog fed!

The problem here is that you are wasting so many opportunities to exercise and train your dog, their food time is a great time to use some of that extra energy and to teach them those manners you would like to see each day.

More than that it can also come down to what you are feeding them. Remember what goes in must come out and I don't just mean from the rear end! The sugars and proteins you put into your dog will come out in their behaviour and health.

A great starting point is to feed the natural rainbow (not coloured kibble), add, veg, fruit, meats as many different things as you can to keep them from becoming bored with their food but also to feed their brain (well actually two brains!). Dogs like us have two brains not just one, the brain found in their head as you would of course expect but also the gut!

The gut is often referred to as the second brain as it has direct links to the brain and how the brain acts, keeping the gut healthy and well fed affects the behaviour of your dog as well of course as their health.

In the wild dogs will scavenge and hunt, this includes eating the stomachs of their prey, here they will find berries, fruits, grass, veg all sorts and we can use this to our advantage. Personally I feed my dogs a raw diet which consists of different meats, bones, fruit and vegetables to ensure they have a healthy varied diet.

I am not a canine nutritionist so I won't go into huge detail as that is not my area of expertise and I am not qualified to do so.

What I will say is there are some amazing people out there who are, but make sure to check what qualifications, accreditations and experience they have (don't just pop on Google and hope for the best).

On that note be aware, many dog food producers will use marketing and pretty colours of their dog food to make it more appealing to us humans! We see these lovely colourful bits of kibble and fancy packaging (often said to be recommended by so and so) but that doesn't mean that food is good for your dog! Check the ingredients, do some research and learn what really is good for your dog.

A website I personally use to check what is in the dog food I feed is called All About Dog Food (www.allaboutdogfood.co.uk I often check this website out to see how my intended dog food is rated, I of course can't recommend it as I am not qualified in this area but it's what I use personally (and of course that may change in the future).

Look for food that is high in natural content, limit the amount of additives in the food (like food colourings and e-numbers you may be aware of for your children), expensive doesn't always mean great value or better ingredients, it can mean better marketing but as a rule of thumb dog food that is more expensive is likely to better for your dog.

Side note: please don't ever feed your dog rawhide, this is a really dangerous type of chew that includes many nasties (do a bit of research and you will see what I mean).

I will never lecture anyone on what to feed your dog, what I will say is what works for you and your dog is best for you and your dog. We all have to take into account price so feed the best you can afford

Feeding your dog

How you feed your dog plays a huge part in their welfare, just popping it down in a bowl will get the job done, but you are missing out on some great ways to enrich your dogs life and to use up some of that extra energy.

Scatter feeding

The easiest way to enrich your dog's life! Whilst I always thought this was cheating for many years I have found so much value in it and so do my dogs.

Take their food out into the garden and throw it in the grass or on the slabs etc (of course make sure it's safe to do so and I don't recommend doing this on gravel and make sure there are not nasty weed killers etc and the area is safe in general and free from rubbish that could harm them as they go searching for their food).

It's that simple, now let your dog out and let them forage for their food, this not only uses up their natural instinct to hunt and forage for food but sniffing is a naturally calming exercise for your dog and will help to calm them down. Bonus points here is that it also helps to keep them satiated (fuller) for longer, and can help to reduce the risk of Bloat (where the stomach fills with gas and can twist - a potentially fatal issue that can be brought on by eating too fast, or being exercised too soon before or after feeding).

If you don't fancy throwing your dog's food outside, do it in the kitchen or another room (this is especially easy for those that kibble feed their dogs).

For those like me that raw feed their dogs, you can do this but it may make a bit of a mess and be a bit smelly in the summer so use a slow feeder bowl, there are many different sorts on the market from those with a spiral to those that I use which look like big stems of grass. Smush the food down and your dog will have to lick around the big blades of plastic to get to their food, this helped my older boy Lazarus who (like a labrador) would wolf his food down in seconds. I actually timed it from a normal bowl to the new puzzle bowl and he went from 1 minute 20 seconds in a normal bowl to nearly 16 minutes in this new puzzle bowl.

Spending nearly 20 minutes eating his food meant that when he had finished he was tired and would happily then go for a rest, it's hard work for that brain working on your dinner for that long but it also follows a much more natural way of eating for dogs picking away at their food instead of just inhaling it.

Enriching our dogs lives

Enrichment

Enriching our dogs' lives should be part of every day with them, after all the only time they get to go out and find their own enrichment is when we take them out. Licki mats, Kong's, hiding their food in paper scrunched up and then placed in a box all helps to use up some of that extra brain power that is especially high in our teen dogs.

One fail safe way to help to use up some brain power when your dog is being a Moo of a dog is to make games for them to complete, hide their food in Kongs, paper, toilet roll middles (with the ends filled over so it just doesn't fall out) and hide these around the house.

Being confined to the house can be a real pain regardless of what the weather is like outside.

Those of you that know me will know I love to give my dog's something to do to entertain their brains and this is where my love of Kong toys comes in! They can be frozen, put through the dishwasher (I know right who knew!) are great for supervised play and my dogs love them.

For my own dogs (who are raw fed) I usually start with a meat 'plug' at the top and then fill with natural yoghurt, finished off with a another meat 'plug', then chuck it in the freezer overnight and voilà the next day its ready to entertain you furry friend.

Don't worry if you kibble feed that's fine too and also makes for a really tasty treat!

Fill your Kong with some bits of kibble and then squeeze some primula cheese in there (most squeezy cheese are fine but make sure you check the ingredients first to make sure there is nothing nasty hiding in there), then squish a few more bits of kibble in there (and if you are feeling really kind maybe some fresh bits of meat like chicken or turkey).

Make sure to fill it nice and compact, after all we don't want it all just dropping out the moment they have it (that's way too easy!).

Pop it in the freezer and the next day you have a great treat that will keep your dog entertained for a good hour or more.

If you don't have a Kong don't panic!

That delivery you had the other day, that screwed up parcel paper, or left over kitchen cardboard tube or egg box are all perfect, along with that cardboard box you keep going to throw out.

Wrap treats (dried are better for this than fresh meat) in pieces of kitchen roll then pop them in the cardboard tube and fold the ends over, then put them in the box

Next get the egg box and pop treats in the little egg cups and close the box

Grab your leftover parcel paper and scrunch it up into a ball about the size of your fist to start off with (you can always go smaller when they know what they are doing but never so small they can eat or swallow it).

Pop all of this into the cardboard box

Close the top and then put it down in front of your dog and encourage them to forage around and find the treats.

Don't forget to always make sure anything you are using for enrichment for your dog is safe and they are supervised at all times.

My food not yours Grrrr!

Resource guarding food

A quick note here, resource guarding (food in particular) can become really dangerous.

Gone are the days (Or so they should be!) when we expected our dogs to be ok with us just taking their bowl or food away from them.

Think of this way, you give me a big slice of cake (chocolate preferably or even better tiramisu, or even coffee and walnut (I am not fussy) but even more so especially if you want me to do something I don't particularly want to do)………..mmmmm cake…………..

Now try and take that off me! I will rise up in the cafeteria and stab you with my plastic spork!

However, offer me some cherry pie instead of the chocolate cake and hey you have one very happy Lillie to give up the cake!

Swapping it out makes it a really nice experience for me, yes I am giving up cake but I am getting cherry pie instead!

If you need to take your dog's food away from them for some reason (it best be a really good reason), make sure you are swapping it out for something even better (e.g. cheese or fresh cooked chicken), BUT don't make this a habit, this is for emergencies only (that chocolate cake had something nasty inside).

The best option here is to add to your dogs food, starting a few feet away from them when you walk past their bowl drop a tasty treat on the floor for them to find, watch their behaviour closely, looking for any kind of freezing, speeding up or staring at you (this means they are really uncomfortable with you being there), as time goes by start to throw the treat slightly closer to them but never put your hand in their bowl, that's their dinner not yours!

Ideally feed your dog somewhere quiet where they can eat their dinner in peace, I feed my dogs when I am about to eat so they are entertained whilst I am eating and we all get to have a peaceful meal (no one wants to be disturbed when they are eating).

If you find that your dog is struggling with this and they let out a growl or guard their food, get a professional in asap to help with this issue!

Hewo

Chapter Ten

Self-employed

Dogs like to have a job they like to have something to do something to entertain their brain and your tenacious teens are definitely in this age bracket. If we don't give a dog something to do they will and I mean they really will find their own work they will become self-employed.

You might think it's great for your dog to become self-employed and self entertaining. You don't need to worry about doing the brain games with them, you don't need to worry about walking them etc because after all they're going to entertain themselves. The problem comes when that self-employment is chewing on your prized possessions. You know the ones, your favourite pair of shoes, your favourite pair of slippers, the door frame, the table leg, the settee, any number of things and that's the problem.

So what can we do to stop the dogs from becoming self-employed? That's pretty easy to be honest with you, although at times it might feel really hard. We need to find something they want to do, something that they really enjoy. With Zeke this is usually training of any kind, he wants to be using his brain. Being a German Shepherd his brain is always on, it never stops, bit like his energy, so I'm forever trying to find new and exciting ways to keep him entertained and to use up his extra brain energy.

As long as he's with me he doesn't really mind what he's doing but what he really really loves is to use his brain. Whether it was work, parkour, obedience training, trick training, anything at all, even practising the basics and going back to puppy exercises he absolutely loves to learn. One of my favourite things to do with Zeke is my 'smart Moo' game of 50 treats.

Smart Moo

It's really really easy, have some treats in little pots around the house.

When I am tottering about the house and I see something I like I give my marker word of 'yes' and reward with a treat.

If he happens to be lying down, he's nice and calm and quiet. I say 'yes' good lad and give him a treat while he's lying down nice and calm. If he's offering me a lovely nice polite sit to say please because he wants something I'll say yes and give him a reward. It's about looking for those little behaviours that we really like and want to see again and catching them, it's as simple as that.

What gets rewarded gets repeated and the great thing about playing the smart Moo game is that it doesn't have to feel like you're making an effort to train your dog, you're just recognising those behaviours you really like and rewarding them as you go along. So always have a tub of treats close by so you don't miss out on an impromptu training moment.

Breed traits

We also need to consider the traits and genetics that come from our dogs breeding. Whilst this is easier when we know the breed of our dog or breeds that make up our mixed breed dog, it can be really hard when we are not sure.

Side note: Genetic testing can be fun but at the moment it's not that reliable, it all depends on how many breeds and how many variations of genetic material the tester has on file. Here you really do get what you pay for, I have known a full pedigree German Shepherd come back as a chihuahua, so buyer beware!

Think of it this way, if you buy a farm bred border collie with parents that have always worked sheep it is highly likely the puppy will have a strong drive to chase and herd (including other dogs, animals and even people and children) so take this into account.

Whilst you may not see these behaviours when they are puppies it will certainly start to increase during their teens! Research your breed preferably before you go out and get your dog but if you already have your dog then now is the time to look at what breed(s) make up your dog and the behaviours you are likely to see from them, this will help to give you a natural outlet for their behaviour. Chasing and herding for example, a flirt pole (a pole with a toy on the end that you can whip around as if it is a small animal) can help to give your dog a natural way to release this energy.

If you have a terrier, atoy that they can drag about will help, if you have a daxie, offer them a safe place to dig such as a childs plastic paddling pool full of sand or dirt. Do some research and look to recreate their breed specific behaviours in a safe way).

Dominance

Dominance is one of the most misused terms in the dog training world and it really gets my goat!

If anyone is dominant it is you not your dog!

We, the humans in this relationship, tell our dogs where they can eat, toilet, walk, play, sleep, sniff. We control practically every moment of their lives.

We shout at them, tell them off for carrying out what are perfectly natural behaviours for them such as chewing, scent marking, running around and chasing after things that move.

If your dog is showing behaviours that you don't like such as pulling on the lead, barking at the neighbour's cat, chewing up your expensive shoes this is your fault, you only have yourself to blame (sorry but it's true). They are not trying to dominate you, they are not trying to be the 'pack leader' , they are not trying to take over the world (that's the cat by the way, they really are looking to take over the world!).

Simply a dog will repeat a behaviour that feels good or gets them a reward, whether that be fuss from the human, eye contact, making you so angry you interact with them just to shut them up (yep shouting at them is just a different type of contact to them but it's still good as you ARE interacting with them), chewing is a naturally rewarding behaviour for dogs and they don't see the difference between a bone and your £1000 shoes, it just feels good, nothing more, nothing less, it feels good. Think of your favourite thing, for me it's chocolate, I know it's going to make me the size of a house but I eat it anyway as it tastes and feels so good!.

Dominance theory

As much as I would prefer not to go down this rabbit hole, I feel we need to very, very, briefly (literally a few lines).

It was long thought that dogs were basically domesticated Wolves and whilst this is true to an extent they have been domesticated for so long now that they are actually a totally different species, don't get me wrong we of course see similarities but they are not wolves.

The origin of the dominance theory came about from a study carried out on captive Wolves and has since been debunked as the wolves were not seen in their natural habitat and hence the observations seen were not indicative of a real wolf pack and its behaviour.

Whilst this is a subject I could go on about for many a page, I won't as there are plenty of brilliant books out there that you may wish to read but this one's for you and unless you are like me and lead a rather uneventful life, consumed by your love of learning, knowledge and especially that relating to canis familiaris you probably won't be that interested in scientific reviews (that's not a bad thing at all I am just a bit of a geek).

Of course if you are fantastic there is literally a lifetime of reading to be had and I will suggest some further reading at the back of this book.

Bath time!

Optimise!

By motivating our dogs and observing their behaviour we really can optimise their training!

Learning what they can and can't cope with, what they do and don't like can really make all the difference!

Take all you have learnt so far and use it to optimise your training with the exercises in the second half of this book

Lazarus is always laughing at me!

Part Five

Where is this chilled out fido you speak of?

Swim time!

Chapter Eleven

Training

The second half of this book is dedicated to simple training exercises that you can do with your dog, even if your dog knows all of these exercises I would really recommend going back to basics.

Dogs when they're in their tenacious teen stage really struggle to understand exercises that they know perfectly well before. You will go through stages where you are absolutely adamant that you did train this dog, you can remember training this dog but you're pretty sure that actually you never trained this dog. Like I say it's like someone swapped your dog overnight and suddenly you have a monster on the end of the lead, raging hormones and energy levels that are just out of this world and let's be honest it's like having a human teenage child in the house but don't worry I'm here to help.

So the best way to work through this part of the book is to follow the flow of exercises, they are in that order for a reason. We want to work up from the simpler exercises to the ones that are a little bit more difficult. We also want to get our dogs' attention back on us before anything else.

That's the most important thing here, getting and keeping our dogs' attention on us and not everything else that's going on around them.

If at any point your dog struggles with any of the exercises don't worry and don't get frustrated, go back a step. If needed go back to the beginning and start again take it slow give them time trying to remember what it was like when you were 15 / 16 and you were in school and the teacher is racing ahead and you're trying to take notes and your brain just can't take it all in and before you know it the class is finished, you came out really frustrated thinking did I learn anything? Generally I was just really bored because when you can't do something well and when you don't understand the task at hand we get bored, we get frustrated and guess what so do our dogs so let's set them up for success!

What do I mean by setting our dogs up for success? We want to make sure that our dogs can win, they can win at the game of training each and every time. We're going to do a little bit of training with them and we're going to make sure that we as much as them are in the right frame of mind. If either of us are in a bad mood or it's just one of those days where you think 'you know what it really isn't the day to train' then that's fine take a day off, take a morning off, take an afternoon off but don't let it become an excuse for not training at all.

Training should be fun not just for our dogs but for us as well and you will hear me say that over and over again.

Another thing you hear me saying over and over is that what gets rewarded gets repeated and this is where you need to be careful.

Training our dogs is a little like trying to train your kids, before you know it you've inadvertently taught them a bad word at a young age, the other half or grandparents are due and your child is saying a bad word, great!

Keep your training sessions short, the time it takes to boil the kettle is the perfect amount of time you don't want to boil the kettle. That's fine, set a timer maximum three minutes at a time! It's really easy to go over time when you're enjoying yourself and you and your dog are having fun but make sure you stop and give them a break especially at this age they need their sleep to allow their brains to take in the training you've just given them. So even if you think things are going really really well and you want to carry on, don't, stop, have a 30 minute break, go back to it if you want to but make sure you and they have a break.

Again, have fun, make sure your dog is having fun, if at any point it stops being fun, stop the training, have a break and come back to it later, I can't emphasise this enough!

Go slowly, give your dogs time to understand, it might be like I say that six months ago they knew it, they could do it, they were perfect but their hormones and their energy levels are making a huge difference now!

Dogs that are in their teenage stage can get frustrated really really quickly. Try to remember back to when you were a teenager and your mum or your dad nagging at you would drive you crazy 'can you do the washing up', 'have you done the washing up', 'will you just do the washing up', 'why haven't you done the washing up', it was really really annoying! This is the same as nagging your dog!

Constantly saying sit, sit, sit, sit, sit whilst your dog is still standing there or moving around being the joker is, I hate to tell you doing nothing but your teaching your dog anything but to 'sit', all you're teaching your dog to do is to wag its bum, wiggle around and be really silly. It's not actually learning to sit, so don't nag your dog. If you feel like you're going to start nagging your dog, stop the training session and come back to it later.

Your dog is going through a really hard time right now, their hormones are raging, their brain is literally changing on a daily basis, trimming the connections they no longer need and mapping out new ones. Think back to when you were a teen it was bloody hard work and you were exhausted all the time (yep I get it, you look back with rose tinted glasses of those long summer nights out with friends and think I wish I had that energy now, but back then your were tired, you needed more sleep and you needed to rest your brain) so does your dog!

Imagine being taught to do a new job and you were constantly told by your new boss that you weren't doing it right, you would get frustrated and give up.

If you are constantly nagged to do something the fun goes out of it and you want to give up. Yet if it is fun and you're paid well, you want to learn and you want to progress!

If at any point you don't feel like right now is the time for you or your dog to train that's fine don't but at the same time don't make it a constant excuse or nothing will ever get done.

Stick to a few 3 minute training sessions a day and you will be amazed at the progress you both make.

Impulse control

Dogs need to learn impulse control and boundaries. It's not easy and as they grow up and their hormones kick in or they become more self-confident they like to push buttons to see what they can and can't get away with. Barking is a great example of this button pushing, they know it gets a reaction from us and this makes it so much more fun!

Impulse control can be used in all areas of our dogs lives, not just at dinner time. Follow these steps to teach your dog that if they wait and have a little patience, whatever it is they want, it will come so much quicker. Of course there will be things they want but they can't have but that's ok too because we have something even better!

Follow these exercises and make sure you do this each and every time, this isn't a one-time magic wand (if only I had one of those!). Just to be crystal clear here if you don't keep up with these exercises and use them consistently you may as well not bother reading on, just give this book to someone who will and say 'here I couldn't be bothered and I just love having a dog that drives me mad, good luck!', harsh but true, training your dog is going to take time, effort, and a lot of patience but I promise it's worth it!

The first thing we are going to teach our dogs is that they will be rewarded for working for us. The way we are going to do this is to show them that when they hear a sound this means the reward is on the way. The reward can be anything from a tasty treat, an ear scratch, a game or play time, to just having fun together or a good belly rub, it's whatever your dog finds rewarding.

What you will need

First of all, I want you to collect up the things you will need to train and work with your dog, don't worry we will go through each point below clearly before you even start to work with the dog.

(Don't worry I will go into much greater detail below so you know exactly what you will need and how to use it).

- Treats
- Clicker (if you don't have one you can pick one up from most pet shops or online for a couple of pounds or you can use your marker word instead)
- The patience of a saint
- A quiet place to practice
- Your dog (obviously)
- A training plan of what you want to teach in this session (don't worry I will give you an example below)
- An idea of what you want from your dog
- The item you are desensitising your dog to (this could be a dog bowl, but can also be their lead, their toys, your shoes etc)
- Regular breaks for you and the dog

Rewards

Many owners I work with worry that their dog will get fat if they use treats, if this is the case just make sure that you take their treat 'allowance' out of their daily food allowance, so if you use say 40g of treats, they have 40g less of their dinner (I don't measure this out I just use common sense).

Another worry is that if the dog works for treats, they will never work without them. Let's just get this out of the way now. I wouldn't go to work for free and I very much doubt you would.

You would expect to be paid.

Treats hold varying value to your dog, that stale old kibble at the back of the cupboard you brought that they never really liked isn't going to hit the spot for your dog and so they aren't going to be thrilled about working for it and will more than likely just ignore you to get what they really want (probably through barking).

A great way to work out which treat your dog likes best is to have a treat off (or toy off if your dog is not a foodie).Select a number of treats (you will need roughly four or five of each for now), make sure you have low to high value treats some great ideas to try with your dog are below:

Their usual dinner (if you kibble feed use a few of these, if you raw feed use a bit of the raw feed)

Cheese

Ham (make sure it's not full of salt - no gammon!)

Turkey

Beef

Dry treats (like the ones you get from the supermarket)

Squeezy cheese (primula is great if you use a different brand make sure it is safe for your dog and no nasty additives, if you're not sure ask your vet), avoid flavours like chilli and chive

Bacon bits (fresh or cooked), again be aware of how much salt is in bacon

Carrot

Peas (don't ask me why but one of mine used to adore peas!)

If you have a dog that isn't into food you can do this with their toys (just replace the treats with toys), you just need to find what makes your dog want to work for you

Make sure you have a good selection as we are going to use these to whittle them down to their top three or four. (Don't forget if your dog isn't into treats thats fine just substitute the word 'treat' for 'toy')

With all your bits of treats to hand, pick the first one up (it doesn't matter in what order you use them).

Throw a treat towards your dog on the floor a little way away from you and them, watch what they do, do they rush over and gobble it up? Do they sniff it and then give it a taste? Do they rush over and go 'bleurgh' I'm not eating that?

We are looking to get a ranking of treats for your dog, keep the ones that they really enjoyed and gobbled up happily to one side (we will rank these again in a minute), for the ones that they weren't too fussed about but still ate put to another side, and the ones that there was no interest in you can get rid of these for now (it may be your neighbour's dog or a friends dog will like them but your dog isn't going to be willing to work for them).

Going back to the ones that they were interested in but not OMG over, throw another one down and see how they react (if there is more than one of these try to rank them on how interested your dog is in them), then repeat this with the OMG treats. We are looking for a ranking system of at least three or four treats going from their number one favourite treat (maybe cheese or turkey for example to their yeah, I'll eat it but I'm not that fussed). Make a note of these (don't forget your dog's tastes may change with time so it never hurts to go back through this process every so often).

Now for the important bit! To quote a very good friend, she like me would do pretty much anything for cake, however, if you were to offer me cake every day for every meal or every time I did something good it would soon lose its appeal to me, so be sparing with your dog's 'cake' you don't want them to lose their love for it.

Treats and toys

Always start off with a high value treat or toy when you're trying a new exercise or you are trying an exercise in a new environment, as the dog gets better at the exercise you can move towards a lower value treat or toy. The aim is here to make new exercises or new environments feel great by offering a really big reward!

Getting ready to train

Let's do this! You've got your treats, you've got your dog, you are in an okay mood (it doesn't have to be a fantastic mood just as long as you're not in a bad mood). Next, where are you going to train? I start off in the house in a nice quiet room where things are nice and relaxed and there is very little distraction. You may think well my dog can do this over the park with 30 other dogs running around and life is great. Well that's fantastic and if you can, hats off to you! But that said, for now to set your dog up for success still start off in your house in a room with very low level distractions (trust me it's worth it).

We want to set our dogs up for success and we want to make sure that they can do these exercises wherever and whenever so going back to basics is always a really good place to start! Even Ezekiel at five years old will go back to basics regularly as this helps the dog to 'proof' the exercise and takes the pressure off them and they find this great fun (we all like a bit of time when things are easier).

Okay we've got the room, we've got the dog, we've got treats, we've got you and we have a plan of action, so now what?

Don't overthink it, just do it, just go with it and see how you get on. If you make a mistake go back a step, if your dog can't do what you've just asked go back a step, if things start to get difficult go back a step. If you need to give you and your dog a break, remember no more than 3 minutes training at a time with at least 30 minutes in between sessions. It really is that simple, don't stress, don't worry it will all come right if you work at it!

Great, you are nearly ready to train your dog.

You will need to find a quiet place to train, if you have other dogs or animals pop them out the way so just you and your dog you are training are in the room.

At first it is best to have just you and the dog you are training in the room so it's free of as many distractions as possible (this includes other people being out of the room where possible for now, or at least asking them to sit quietly to give your dog the best chance of listening to you).

Take a breath and try to relax (your dog can feel your emotions and can hear your heartbeat rising and this will have an effect on their behaviour so try to stay calm – easier said than done I know!).

Always set a timer on your phone, you don't want to be training for any more than three minutes at a time.

Tenacious teens are some of the hardest dogs to train, they are live wires, they either want to do everything at breakneck speed or they are just not interested in anything you have to say and want to pay attention to everything else going on around them, hence the need for a quiet space to train and the patience of a saint!

When you have done just 3 minutes of training go grab a cuppa and relax that's it for right now, let your dog relax, preferably we want them to sleep for at least 30 minutes and then come back and repeat the above no more than 3 times a day for no longer than an absolute maximum of 5 minutes at a time.

There is no point in rushing a tenacious teen all that will do is make you come across as you are 'nagging' them and we all know how that feels!

Hold it! Before we move on, make sure you can tick off all of the above so you're ready to train as soon as you have read the next exercise.

When you are ready, read on…….

No nagging!'

One of the most important things about training is –

IT SHOULD BE FUN!

If you're not having fun and if your dog isn't having fun neither of you are going to learn….simples!

Itsy is always happy

Chapter Twelve

Marker or clicker?

This one is really up to you both can work as well as each other

Marker word

A marker word is a simple word that you use to tell your dog they have done something right. I use 'Yes' as this comes naturally to me and when timing is everything you want something easy to remember and use.

A marker word should be a single syllable word so it's said and heard easily, it taps into that part of your dog's brain that then says 'great a reward is coming'

The great thing about a marker word is it is free however; it can be hard to get the timing right and to actually remember to say 'Yes' when they get something right

Clicker

A clicker acts in the same way as a marker word, it is a small box (sometimes it will look like a button) that has a small metal plate inside that when pressed it makes a 'click' sound. With time and practice this teaches the dog that when they hear the 'click' good things happen (a treat or a toy appear).

Clickers are great and are what I use primarily with my own dogs, the downside is that it's something else to have in your hand and when you already have a lead, treats, and everything else you're trying to figure out it can get a little awkward.

Priming your marker word or clicker

Whether using a marker word or a clicker we first need to 'prime' them, think of it like charging a battery

With your dog in front of you we are going to play the 'name game' (this is a great one for building on your recall with your dog), the main thing to remember here is not to call their name until you are 99% sure they are going to respond to you. A great time to do this is when you're about to put their food down to start with.

Say your dog's name once (no more) and as soon as they look at you say 'Yes' or click and give them a treat

Repeat this at least 10 times (let them become distracted in-between each time).

If your dog doesn't look at you, don't say their name again, instead make yourself really fun to be with – make kissy noises, get all excited and wave your arms around, be silly!

As they look at you say 'Yes' or click and give them a treat

Voila you have primed your marker word or treat, now make sure to do this at least once a day for the next ten days

Reward schedules

Next we are going to look at reward schedules, you may think at first how on earth can I keep up with giving them soooo many treats they are going to be the size of a bus!

Don't worry it won't always be this way but at first yep we need to make it really rewarding for them.

Think of it like this, you are told by your boss that you have to learn a new route to drive. You're really panicking, you can't even understand the words they are using, let alone where you're supposed to be going!

Option one: Your boss decides the best way to get you to do this is to leave you to it, no instructions, no help, no map!

You spend the next 30 minutes trying to work out where the hell it is your going let alone how to get there!

You get really stressed and to top it off your boss is shouting at you for being late!

Option two: Your boss decides to help you, they give you a map with a big cross of where you need to get to, and the points to stop off along the way and they give you a rough idea of the roads to take.

You set off in a car with fuel, a sandwich to keep you going and some tunes to keep you happy.

The best bit is when you get to the stops along the way you will be rewarded with a cuppa and at the end of the route you get a big slice of homemade cake!

Which option would you prefer? I know which option I would prefer!

It's the same for our dogs, when we are teaching them something new we need to be rewarding them frequently. When they get to a point where they are on the way to getting the new exercise we need to reward them, when they do really really well (for example they sit in a really distracting place we need to jackpot reward them!)

When we start out on a new cue or exercise with our dogs we need to make sure we are making it worth their while, we don't like to work for free and neither do they.

Reward your dog each and every time they get it right, if they don't get it right that's ok, they don't get a reward for that attempt.

As they start to get the idea you can start to randomise when they get a reward. When your dog can carry out the exercise 3 times in a row, for three consecutive sessions, you can start to offer a reward for every 2nd or 5th or 3rd or 6th time they get it right. It's amazing how when we vary how often our dogs get a reward just how much harder they will work for it. A word of warning though! Each time you increase the Duration, Distance or level of Distractions (3 D's) you need to up the amount of rewards you are giving them to each and every time again, until you guessed it they can do it each and every time three times in a row for three consecutive sessions.

To teach your dog a new cue there are two main ways we can do this, through luring and shaping, it's important to understand the difference as this can really help you to find new and inventive things to teach your dog.

Luring

When we lure our dog we use something for them to follow (usually a treat) . You will see this most commonly when teaching the sit or the down cue or lead walking.

We pop a tasty treat on the end of their nose and ask them to follow it, for example asking them to follow the treat for a step or two before rewarding them with that treat to teach them how to walk nicely on lead.

Whilst luring is great in the beginning when teaching a new cue we need to be able to move away from this pretty quickly (after all if you have a small dog you will be bending down so you can reach their nose with the treat will leave you with a bad back).

Shaping

Shaping is another option and a great one with teens in particular! Their brains become tired very quickly and so they may not always be able to perform an exercise all in one go.

Asking your dog to follow a treat from their nose to their toes to encourage them to lie down may not be as easy as you think, the front end goes down, the bum pops up and vice versa.

With a mix of luring and shaping we are going to reward the dog for increments of the desired behaviour, then when they get the whole behaviour we are going to jackpot them with a number of treats in one go.

A great example of luring and shaping is teaching the down, like discussed above this can be a really hard one for teens to remember what to do and it isn't a natural position for dogs to go into.

We start by luring them with treats from their nose to toes. Instead of waiting for their whole body to go onto the floor we are going to reward little sections and each time they get that we are going to ask for a little bit more.

It goes a bit like this:

Step one:

Treat on the dogs nose, we take the treat in our hand toward their front toes, the dog lowers its head, we reward that action.

Step two:

Next time we take the treat from the dogs nose towards their front toes but we look for them to bend their front end slightly more towards the floor, we reward this.

Step three:

Look for their front feet to move forwards ready to go into a down and reward this and so on until the dog goes fully into the down, as soon as they are in the down with their whole body we jackpot reward them whilst they are in that position with one treat after another to make that position really worthwhile repeating.

Using the shaping method means they are rewarded for each little attempt in the right direction, making it easier for them to understand what we want them to do. Once we have them going all the way to the floor we can then ask for this in one go and voila you have a down!

Cue word

What is a cue word?

A cue word is a signal to the dog that we want them to carry out a specific behaviour for example when we ask for them to 'sit' their bum goes to the floor and they sit quietly until we release them or ask them to do something else

When do we use a cue word?

When we are first teaching the dog a new behaviour, we don't put a word or cue to it until the dog can do the behaviour reliably, there are two reasons for this:

Firstly, when the dog is learning to carry out the exercise, we want them to concentrate on the behaviour, there is no point trying to put the cue to the behaviour at this point as the dog doesn't understand what we are looking for yet

Secondly, we want to ensure that the cue is only associated with the finished behaviour, we don't want to teach them that 'sit' means messing about and then eventually put your bum on the floor, we want them to know that when we say 'sit' your bum goes to the floor and you stay in the sit until they are released or asked to do something else

Introducing a cue word

Repeat the steps above but this time use your 'cue' word immediately before you ask for the new behaviour.

For example with the 'Sit'

Pop a treat on the end of their nose and raise your hand upwards, their head comes up and their bum goes down into a sit, great! Well done! Treat held in front or sat on their nose

Next time, say 'Sit' immediately before you raise your hand to cue their bum to go to the floor and reward them when their bum hits the floor.

Proofing

So now your dog can offer a 'sit' . We are going to 'proof' this stage so far (proofing is the dog training term for making sure they can give the behaviour regardless of where they are or what is going on around them).

Next time you train this exercise increase the criteria you are asking for but always follow the three D's

Duration

Distractions

Distance

Duration

First, we are going to ask them to increase the time they remain on the sit for.

Now when you ask your dog to sit, you are going to ask them to hold that position for a few seconds at a time before you click and treat.

Make sure you vary how long you ask them to hold the sit for, you can follow the below if this helps:

1 second, 2 seconds, 3 seconds, 5 seconds, 2 seconds, 6 seconds, 7 seconds, 4 seconds, 6 seconds, 7 seconds, …..and so on……

Varying the time, you ask them to remain in the sit for help them to stop getting bored and teaches them not to pre-empt how long you want them to sit still for.

Distractions

Secondly, we are going to ask them to do this somewhere there are more distractions, this could be in the back garden (birds singing, wind, people milling about outside, the noise of the cars etc are all distracting to your dog)

Don't go too fast, if you go somewhere with distractions and the dog can't sit for even a second or two you have gone too fast. Go back indoors to a less distracting place and practice a bit more. Then try again.

An example of distracting environments maybe as below:

Lounge

Kitchen

Back garden

Front garden

Outside on your drive

Just outside of your house on the street

Further down your street

On their walk

Over the park

Somewhere new

Don't forget if you go somewhere to train and you can't get your dog to sit, you have gone too fast, go back a step and try again.

Once you can get your dog to sit and to remain in the sit for five seconds and they can do this even in distracting environments then you can start to add distance.

Distance

Start as you have before with the dog in front of you and take a step backwards. Does your dog remain in the sit or do they come towards you?

If they remain in place for one second go back to them and reward them, if they move towards you, too bad no reward this time and try again, this time just go back a step and maybe rock on leg and reward them for remaining in the sit.

Learning distances

We need to understand and be aware of learning distances for our dogs as these affect how they will behave and how they will cope with the distractions around them.

Too far away:

The distraction is so far away that your dog isn't even aware of it They won't learn to ignore it, as they aren't aware of it

Aware but relaxed: Ideal

Your dog knows the distraction is there but isn't worried about it, they are looking at it but then looking away (preferably back at you), relaxed body posture

This is the best place to be, they are aware but still relaxed in their environment

Too close: Over threshold

Your dog has seen the distraction and is really aware of it, tense body posture, staring, lunging, barking, dog may try to pull towards it or away from it - no learning opportunities here they won't, (or rather can't) look back at you, or if they do its for a split second before you lose their attention again)

Stay in the ideal learning distance

Aware but relaxed

Your dog is aware of the squirrel/other dog / person etc they can see it and / or hear it but they are relaxed, soft and relaxed body posture.

If your dog starts to freeze and stare, give them more space between them and the distraction (this will change each time depending on your dog's mood and the distraction, even the same distraction on another day may cause more / less of a reaction).

Ideally they will look towards the distraction but then look around / look at you there is no freezing of their body or hard stare, they are happy to 'Look, look back'

This is where they will learn the most. Practice some really easy exercises with them such as their sit, down and stand, it may feel like you are re-teaching the exercise (you are!). They need to learn that they can still work for you even when they are distracted, this is where your high value treats come in really handy!

As your dog gets better with distractions they will start to look at you instead of the distraction, knowing when they do look at you instead of the distraction, good things happen (making the distraction less and less of a distraction and your attention even more rewarding).

Ziggy at 16

Chapter Thirteen

Let's train!

The first exercise I always teach with a tenacious teen is the 'watch me', this is your bread and butter exercise, the one I use even more than sit or down!

This is the exercise that will help you no end, however for a tenacious teen it is hard, really hard, especially as their brains are constantly firing with all the other things they could be getting up to, you know chasing squirrels, barking at the neighbour's cat, winding you up in their lead, the list goes, on……..

Whilst the 'watch me' exercise may feel really basic to you and your dog it is one that can't be overlooked, it is one the best exercises for getting your dog to just 'relax' and look at you.

Used correctly it can help your dog to calm themselves even in the most distracting of environments and can make the difference between a dog that wants to run off and play with everyone else to one that wants to be with you the 'great holder of the good stuff'.

All we are asking for is for the dog to look at you and to maintain that eye contact with you regardless of what is going on around them, sounds simple right! Well it is, but then again think about when you were a teen yourself, your mom or dad would call you and ask you to do a chore and give you instructions, did you listen? Or did you get distracted by pretty much anything else going on instead? This is your dog now so we need to show them that having their attention on you is the most amazing thing ever, and good things come to those that pay attention.

Note: we are not going to use your dog's name just yet!

We just want to get your dog's attention on you, and as we know this is easier said than done!

Watch me

Step one:

With a treat (or toy) in your hand, put the treat under their nose

When they look at you 'click' and give a treat (even if they just glance at you 'click' and give a treat)

If you are struggling to get your dog's attention make kissy noises, wave your arms about anything to get their attention (but don't say their name), you may feel like a bit of a fool but if it works use it (you know what they say dance as if no one is watching), then 'click' and give a treat.

Step two:

Throw a treat off to the side to encourage the dog to move away from you then repeat the steps above 3 times

Don't forget you may need to use one of their top-ranking treats at first to really get their attention and then as they find this exercise easier you can start to use lower ranking treats (or toys) until you try this in a new environment.

Step three:

If you can now get your dog's attention with the treat / toy or by making kissy noises great, if not repeat another 3 times and keep doing this until you have got them reliably looking at you're for the treat or toy making sure you click and treat each time they do BUT remember to not go over 3 minutes per session at a time!

Step four:

When they can reliably look at you and hold that attention then start to vary when and what treats they get.

Ask them to hold their attention on you, click but NO treat

Release the dog by throwing a treat off to the side

Do this again but this time giving a click and treat when they have reached the criteria you are looking for (hold attention to you for 2/6/10 seconds, change it up each time).

Sit to say please

The Sit to say 'please' is really easy and honestly comes in so handy in so many situations.

Simply, we are going to teach the dog that if they want something the best and quickest way to get it is to sit and say please. Now you might think well that's easy, surely, I just ask them to sit when they are being a tenacious idiot, but generally this isn't going to work for you I am afraid.

For a start they have no idea what you are actually asking them for, sure they more than likely know how to sit but sitting to say please is something different, it takes patience on your part and on the dog's.

For now, we are going to work on their dinner bowl as this is one of the most common points at which your dog will get over excited.

Step one:

First of all, we need to desensitise your dog to the thing that is making them over excited in this case their dinner bowl.

Pick up your dog's bowl, if they get excited and bark, don't react, just hold the bowl in your hand. We are now going to ignore everything else they do and wait for them to sit, when their bum hits the floor, reward them with a piece of their dinner from the bowl.

Step two:

Repeat this for everything they want, whatever they want they need to sit to say please calmly first before they get access to it, whether this be fuss, dinner, play time etc. Every time they want something they sit to say please first, this will help them to stay calm and will keep all four paws on the floor.

Swap it

Great so now your dog can ask politely for what they want. Next we need to help them to understand there are times we may need to take something away from them.

Dogs really enjoy their prized possessions as we do, we need to teach our dogs that there are times when we need to take things off them.

Make sure you have a number of toys / chews available ready next to you (in a bag or such like can be handy so they don't try to take them all in one go) put them in your reach, but not in reach of your dog.

Step one:

Get one of your dog's toys and get them interested in it, let them win by allowing them to hold onto the toy and have a gentle game of tug of war making sure they are allowed to win occasionally and hold onto the toy.

Step two:

Let them play with the toy for about 10 seconds and then offer them another toy to play with, making sure the second toy is even more interesting, imagine how a squirrel behaves it doesn't run up to the dog and boop it on the nose, it darts around, runs close and then dashes away, stopping for a second or two along the way (mimic a squirrel with the toy).

When they drop the first toy to go after the second, wait a few seconds, let the dog 'win' the second toy and then pick up the first.

Step three:

Now repeat with different toys, each time allowing the dog to have time to enjoy the toy (we don't want to stop them from having something to play with just to show we may have to swap it at times).

Step four:

You can also swap out chews this way, let them have their chew. Then offer them something even better such as a piece of fresh meat or cheese, when they drop the chew, pick it up, wait for them to finish the treat and then give the chew back to them, each time extending the time by a couple of seconds before they get their chew back by offering them a further treat whilst they wait.

If your dog doesn't want to give up their toy or chew and they are growling, be careful, they are trying to tell you it is theirs and they don't want you to have it. Listen to them, don't try to just take it away.

If this happens try to up the value of what you are swapping their toy or chew for (this is where you hierarchy of treats and toys comes in, so if they are more interested in the chew than a bit of kibble bring out the big money – cheese or meat is usually good salary change). You need to make sure that the thing you are offering them in exchange for the thing they have is better (much better) to make it worth their while.

Note: If your dog really doesn't want to give up what they have, speak to your trainer as it may be you need to do some more work around this. Most of all be careful taking items away from your dog, and reward when they do give it up.

Leave it

The 'leave' cue is a great cue and can help you to keep your dog safe, this cue comes in really handy over the park after a Friday night where there may be left over food from the night before hanging around.

It is also a great cue that can be used in cafés or pubs where there may be food on the floor and is really useful at home when you don't want your dog stealing food off the table

First of all, we are going to teach the leave from the hand

Food in the hand

Step one:

Put a treat in your hand and fold your fingers around it to make a fist

Show your hand to the dog, they may sniff or nibble at your hand to get to the treat

Wait for your dog to take their nose / mouth away from your hand. As soon as they do, mark with 'yes' then offer them the treat, if they try to snaffle your fingers, fold you're your fingers around the treat again

A little word of warning, dog teeth are very sharp so when you give the dog a treat do so from the palm of your hand if needed so they can't nip at your hand

Step two:

Repeat the above until you can hold your hand in front of your dog and they stop and wait to be offered the treat

Once they can do this reliably, you can add your cue word of 'leave' immediately before you show them your hand with the treat in your closed hand

Moving on

Once they can do this from a closed hand, try with your hand open and only closing your fingers around the treat if they try to take it.

Food bowl

Step one:

With your dog sitting in front of you and their food bowl in your hand (make sure there is something yummy in the bowl for them) slowly lower the bowl down a few inches away from your dog.

If they dash to try to get to the food, lift the bowl up and start again.

We are aiming here to get the bowl all the way to the floor with the dog still in the sit..

Step two:

Once the bowl is on the floor and they are still in the sit, give your release word and let them have what's in the bowl (the bowl in this case is their reward).

Step three:

Do this every time you feed them and then build up the time they are in the sit before they are released to bowl, eventually counting up to ten before they can eat.

Food on the floor

Put a treat on the floor and carefully cover it with your foot.

As soon as your dog takes their attention from the treat on the floor say 'yes', pick the treat up off the floor.

Give a treat from your hand (do not let them have the treat from the floor).

(Don't worry that they are not getting the treat from your hand straight away your marker word of 'yes' tells them a treat is coming, a few seconds delay is fine).

Repeat x 5

Build this up until you can put a treat on the floor without your foot covering the treat at all with your dog sitting still and waiting for 5 seconds before you say 'yes' and give a treat from the hand (not the one on the floor).

Touch

There are times when we need to be able to move our dogs and the easiest way to do this is to teach the hand touch, this is a really useful cue for when we need to get the dog off the settee or off the bed.

We are going to teach your dog to put their nose to your hand and 'boop' it so that we can put our hand out, ask for the touch and the dog will move to come to you and touch your hand with their nose.

Step one:

Start with your dog sitting by you, then put your hand by the side of your dog's face (not on their face), with your palm facing their face, don't say anything or make any noise.

We are looking for them to investigate the middle of your palm with their nose, we will build this up to a 'touch'.

As soon as they turn to look and investigate mark with 'Yes' and reward with a treat

Repeat x 5

Step two:

Repeat this and each time, wait for them to give a little more and mark with 'Yes' and reward with a treat. Build it up slowly like below:

- Turning to look at your hand
- Turning and sniffing your hand
- Turning and sniffing your hand but with a little more pressure with their nose
- Booping your hand with their nose

Repeat this with you putting your hand close to them:

- Each side
- Slightly in front of them
- Slightly to the side and behind

Remember to mark with 'Yes' and reward with a treat each time they investigate your hand at first and then ask for a nose boop before your mark and reward and build up the length of contact as you go

Give your dog a break! This is hard work after all

Step three:

Next, we are going to start again but this time we are only going to mark 'Yes' and reward you with a treat when they push their nose into your palm and hold it there. Start with just pressing their nose to your hand for one second. Then build this up following the steps you have just taken so that they can then hold their nose to your hand for 5 seconds.

Once you have reached this stage, we are going to add the cue word of 'Touch'

Step four:

Start step three again but this time immediately before you put your hand out say the cue word 'touch', if they get it right mark with 'Yes' and reward with a treat

Build this up so that when you say 'touch' they put their nose to your palm and hold it there for a few seconds until you give your release word.

Once we have got to the point where they can hold their nose in place for 5 seconds, we are going to build the distance they can do this from.

Well done you are doing great! This may feel a long process but for such a useful cue it is worth it!

Step five:

With your dog sitting in front of you move one pace away

Put your hand out and ask for a 'touch' if they get it right mark with 'Yes' and reward with a treat

Now try two steps away, then three, then four, then two steps to the side

Keep building on this so that eventually wherever your dog is (settee, bed, anywhere where you need to move them) you can put your hand out and ask for a 'touch' and they will come to you to boop your hand

Chapter Fourteen

The magic portal to Narnia!

Door control

Any of the below sound familiar?

Dashing to get out of the door where your dog literally forgets you are there and barges past you?

Excitement so palpable when you come through the door that they literally can't stay still?

You pick up the lead and the whole world is lost to chaos?

What your dog needs is some impulse control and generally this is something dog owners rarely do, after all it is so much easier to just give in and give the dog whatever it is they want so they stop barking and driving the neighbours nuts!

Does your dog lose their mind over their lead?

Most do and this is something that we can work on together.

The biggest reason your dog loses their mind whenever you go near the lead is simple really, when the lead goes on 99%

of the time it means they are off out for a walk, maybe a run and best of all they get to do this with you, it's the sign of great fun is about to be had

From day one when you brought your dog home their lead has meant you are off out with them so now the lead

Let's start by showing your dog their lead doesn't' always mean walkies, after all it may be you just need to move the lead

We are going to show your dog that calm behaviours get rewarded and excited behaviours do not.

A quick note on rewarding your dog:

If your dog stays calm, reward them with a calm voice and a treat (calm behaviours are rewarded).

If your dog gets over excited, wait for them to calm down and then reward them with a calm voice but **NO** treat.

We want to reward them for calming down but we also want to show them that calm behaviours around the lead are what we are looking for.

Now don't get me wrong we are not looking for your dog to stay asleep but a nice sit to say please will do, after all going for a walk is exciting.

Follow these steps to help your dog understand that the lead doesn't always mean walkies but if they stay calm it will at least mean good things come their way like treats.

Make sure you set a timer if needed (or if you, like me, use the kettle boiling as your timer), you want these training sessions to be no longer than two / three minutes at a time.

Always start with step one, as you progress you will forget these are actual steps and it will become natural but following the steps below one by one for now will make sure you don't slip into bad habits again and will help your dog to learn consistency is key!

If it helps explain to the others in your household that for now only you will handle the lead and then eventually you will show them how to work through the below themselves so the dog is calm regardless of who picks up the lead.

If at any point you move up a step and your dog becomes excited again, go back a step, take it slow it's worth it!

Step one:

Stand still, pick up the lead, if your dog comes dashing towards you, put it back down.

Repeat the above until you can pick up the lead and your dog stays calm. Each time they stay calm reward them with a calm voice and treat.

Step two:

Pick up the lead and move about a little just (one or two steps will do for now), if your dog gets excited put the lead back down.

Repeat the above until you can pick up the lead and move a couple of steps with your dog staying calm.

Step three:

Pick up the lead and move towards the dog, if your dog is now dashing around you and jumping put the lead back down.

Repeat until you can pick up the lead and move towards your dog with them staying calm.

Step four:

Pick up the lead and move towards your dog and go to clip the lead on if they stay calm, clip the lead on and stay calm, then remove the lead and reward them.

Repeat until you can pick up the lead and clip it on with the dog staying calm.

If at any point you move up a step and your dog becomes excited again, go back a step, take it slow.

You are doing great! You have in no time at all taught your dog to be calm around their lead, you can now pick it up, put it down, attach it to the dog, take it off and all the time they are calm, really well done this is no small feat!

So what's next?

Next we have to get to the door, it's funny isn't it you never realised there were so many steps to just going for a walk with your dog!

It may seem like you are never going to get on this walk but you will and when you do it will be so much easier!

OK so we have the lead on the dog, the dog is calm you are calm, so now we are going to head towards the door but wait, the dog is now spinning like a top and pulling on the lead arghhhh.....

We want to keep our dog calm ready for the walk so if your dog is now too excited, stand still and become bored, sit down if it is easier, wait for them to calm and then try again.

A calm dog is a happier dog on a walk so we want them to be calm before we leave the house. You are rocking this!

You have worked through the excitement of the lead and heading towards the door, now to tackle getting through the door!

The door, that great pinch point where owner and dog become one merging into another at the same time to get through that wonderful portal to the outside!

Same rules apply here as above, if your dog gets excited by the door take it slow, just touch the door handle first, if they stay calm, reward, if they get excited wait for them to calm down and then try again, little tiny increments is the way forward and make sure you follow this each and every time you pick up their lead or head for the door.

A dog that isn't calm doesn't have its lead put on until it is calm and you don't go through the door until they are calm the whole way through and out the other side.

Great! Well Done! You have made it out of the door! Now what?

Look, Look back (Check in)

We are going to teach our dogs that it is ok to look at what has got their attention but then we want their attention back on us.

We aim to use the 'look, look back' at the point of the distraction catching their attention. We don't want our dogs to be so close that it is worrying them or they are now over excited as they cannot learn at this point. This is the time when we would say they are over threshold

Each time they see a distraction let them look at it and then ask them to look at you and reward for making eye contact with you

We are now going to build up the time their attention is on you but do this slowly, the main thing here at first is to teach them that it is ok to look at the distraction, but then they have to look back at you and give you their attention

Simple rules:

- Only ever let them look at the distraction for 2 seconds at a time, then they need to look back at you

- If they won't look back at you, move them further away and try again, don't tell them off just be more exciting than the distraction to get them to follow you

- Don't use their name, make kissy noises, squeak anything to get their attention but not their name

- Remember there are a number of reasons why they are distracted and that will be holding their attention so you need to be more appealing than the distraction

- If your dog is scared show them that you will protect them and take them away from what is scaring them, never force them to 'face' their fears this will only backfire and make them even more scared

Recall – name game

A good recall could one day save your dog's life, it is one of the most important cues to teach.

To start we are going to use the name game

Do

- Only use your dog's name when you are at least 99% sure they are going to come straight back to you

  - When you think their attention is about to be on you, say their name in a high pitched and excited voice

- As soon as they look at you show them you are really excited

- The moment they get back to you, make a big fuss of them and give them a treat. Reward every time, no matter if you are in the house, the garden or the park and no matter how long it takes them to come back to you

Now let's make it a little harder

Put some toys out around the house and then repeat the above. Do the same in the garden.

- Out and about only let your dog off if you are 100% sure you can get them back to you

- You can ask someone else to help you by calling the dog between you, start with very short distances and build up. Make sure each person is excited as the other and gives fuss, rewards and gives a treat each and every time the dog comes back to you

If you can hire a secure field this is a great place to start

Don't

- Forget to reward your dog each time they come back to you, no matter how long it has taken them to come over to you

- Let your dog off in an open space that isn't secure until you are 100% sure you can get them back to you

- Remember you need to be more exciting than everything else going on including that pesky squirrel!

Time off lead is your dog's biggest reward so you need to make sure you're even better than time off lead!

Whistle recall

A whistle is a great back up for recall (and can be used instead of using their name if you want to). For me it is my emergency recall.

The same as marker words and clickers we are going to teach our dog that a whistle means good things are on the way

Week one:

Each time you're about to give your dog their dinner you use the whistle first.

Two blasts on the whistle and then let the dog have its dinner.

Week two:

With your dog in another room (but with the doors open so they can get to you) Repeat as for week one but this time they need to come to you to get to the food

If your dog is always with you when you make their dinner up, throw a treat into the other room once their dinner is made and ready to give to them, as soon as they have eaten the treat, blow the whistle and then put their dinner down for them

Week three:

Carry on as with week two but now try letting them in the garden first so they have to come in from the garden to get their dinner when the whistle blows.

(Always make sure your dog hasn't been running around too much outside or in the house before feeding them, a little run into the house should be fine but don't feed an out of breath / exercised dog and don't let them run around after eating either – always aim to leave at least half an hour between exercise and feed times)

Week four:

Carry on as week three but this time you're not going to give them their dinner instead they get a tasty treat.

By now they should know what it means but if not keep practising and go back a step for a few days.

Set your dog up for success:

Only use the whistle to call your dog if you are 99% sure they are going to come to you, if they are chasing that pesky squirrel outside, or a visitor has just arrived and they are saying hello, wait until their attention is off that first and don't rush the process. Take your time it's worth it and don't forget that the outside world is a big exciting place so calling your dog back with a whistle when they are off playing with friends is going to take a lot of practice – only use it when you are sure they are going to come back to you first time or you they will lose interest in the whistle and it will become background noise to them.

Loose lead walking

Loose lead 300 peck game

When we look at teaching loose lead walking with the 300 peck system, our only criterion is that the lead must be slack when we reach the count.

It doesn't matter what else the dog is doing when the count is reached (sniffing the floor, looking at you, wagging tail etc.) the only important thing is that the lead is slack. If the lead isn't slack when the count is reached, then the count is reset to 1.

The process looks something like this:

Step one:

Begin with the food reward in your hand by the dog's nose so that the dog is aware that it is there.

With your dog on lead take one step forward, if the lead remains slack say 'Yes' and reward with a treat.

Step two:

Now repeat taking two steps, then three, four and so on until you reach 300 (ok so it doesn't have to be 300 but you get the idea).

Note:

If the dog goes ahead of you or behind you and the lead becomes tight, go back to the beginning and start off with one step again.

You will probably get 3 or 4 steps before the dog tightens the lead and you reset the count.

You may have to reset the count several times before you progress past a count of 10.

You may walk 85 steps or more in order to achieve that count of 10 in the beginning, but as the dog gets the idea; it will begin offering the behaviour more frequently and readily.

As your dog gets better at it you can start to increase the criteria by a count of 10 instead of a count of 1.

One trouble spot seems to be around the 60-70 mark, keep going it is worth it, just remember to say the steps out loud and mark and reward frequently especially in the beginning

Loose lead drunk walking

So you may feel a little silly doing this one but it really works!

It's best to try this in your house or garden first so you can get used to how it feels and to encourage your dog to follow you with no distractions.

Step one:

With your dog on a lead, start to move around, if your dog follows you say 'yes' and reward, at this time all we are looking for is for the dog to follow us on a nice loose lead.

Step two:

Take a step to the side, if the dog follows you with a nice loose lead say 'yes' and reward.

The main aim here is to not take more than three steps in any one direction with the dog walking with you on a nice loose lead (hence the name drunk walk).

Loose lead lampposts

Another option to teach your dog how to walk loosely on a lead is to use the lampposts or other mark points on your walk.

Step one:

From the first lamppost to the second you are going to ask your dog for a loose lead (perhaps using the 300 peck system or drunk walk).

Step two:

From the second to the third lamppost they get to be a dog, sniffing and taking in the environment around them (but still no tension on the lead).

Step three:

From the third lamppost to the fourth they need to walk loosely on lead again.

Do this for all of your walk, it sounds tiring but it really helps the dog to know there is a time for sniffing and being a dog and a time for walking with you.

Next time you go out for a walk double it:

Lamppost one to three they need to walk with you on a loose lead Lamppost three to five they get to sniff (still no tension on the lead though) and so on....

Each time you go for a walk vary which lampposts they get to be a dog between and which they walk with you for as we don't want them to start to only walk between say the first and third, fifth and seventh lampposts on a loose lead and expect to be free to be a dog in between those.

Step four:

Now repeat this over and again but each time take a step in a different direction, remember to say 'yes' and reward each time the dog follows you and has a nice loose lead.

Now start to take a few steps in any direction but keep changing direction as you go, we want to teach our dogs that there is no point in anticipating where we are about to go as it is random.

This helps to keep the dog listening to us, they are never sure which way we may go next and so they need to stay with us on a nice loose lead.

Taking this out and about on a walk can feel a bit strange but it can still easily be done.

Head off on your walk, but instead of just walking the same route as always, cross the road (when it's safe to do so of course), walk a little way then cross over again.

Then perhaps turn around and go back the way you came, then turn around again and go back the original way.

Even walking your usual route the other way round can make a huge difference!

Wait

Wait is simply a cue to the dog to wait where they are, we will tell them what to do next. This is a really handy cue especially for going through doors or if we need to go up the stairs first or for anytime where just need the dog to stay still for a moment before we do something else

The wait cue can be used in any position. Let's start with the sit:

We want to show our dogs that when they just sit and wait, they get rewarded.

Step one:

With your dog in the sit, stand in front of them and feed them treats one after another x 3.

Step two:

Now take half a step back and repeat giving them a treat one at a time x 3. If they get up at any point, ask them to sit and try again, don't forget if they get up more than once in a row, go back a step and keep practising that step for a little while longer.

Step three:

Now take one step back and give treats x 3. Go back to your dog and praise for waiting in the sit, then throw a treat to the side to reset your dog.

Give your dog a break and then come back later for the next session:

Step four:

Start with your dog in front of you and you one step backwards away from them, then feed them a treat one after another x 3. Now take two steps back and repeat. Now take a step to the right and repeat and then to the left and repeat.

Go back to your dog and praise for waiting in the sit then throw a treat to the side to reset your dog.

Step five:

Follow the above until you can take 2 steps away from them in any direction (at this distance you should still be able to give them treats at arm's length one after another). Now the dog knows what we expect from them we are going to put our cue word to it of 'wait'

Step six:

Start again from the beginning this time adding the cue word of 'wait' immediately before you take a step back and then feed 3 treats whilst they wait in the sit position.

If they get up at any point, ask them to sit and try again, don't forget if they get up more than once in a row, go back a step.

Step seven:

Now we are going to make this a little harder by taking this to a new environment. Start to put your dog in the sit in different rooms of the house and cue them to wait and then take it into the garden and build it up slowly. Each time go back to your dog, if they are still in the sit throw a treat to the side and end with lots of praise and a game!

Settle

The 'Chill' or 'settle' cue is used when we are out and about perhaps at a café or pub and we want our dogs to relax

Similar to the 'bed' cue as in we want our dogs to relax but generally we don't use a bed (after all I can't see anyone wanting to really carry their dogs bed around with them) it is also generally used whilst the dog is on the lead as they are out of the home.

Note: This is the one exercise where when we use the marker word, we do so lightly and softly. The sound of a marker word is exciting to your dog as it means something good is on the way so we are going to whisper it soothingly

Teaching the settle:

You need to sit somewhere you can be comfortable as we are going to teach this exercise with us sitting and relaxing.

Step one:

Guide your dog into a down with your hand but don't give the 'down' cue and place or gently throw a treat so that it is next to their back thigh between their leg and abdomen.

As the dog turns to get the treat they should roll onto one hip and be in a relaxed down position (if they stay in a sphynx like pose resting on four legs as if they can jump up at any moment, place or throw another treat a little further in towards their abdomen so they roll onto one hip).

This relaxed position on their hip / side is a much more stable position for the dog and will help them to relax instead of being ready to stand or jump up.

Once they are in this position:

Step two:

With your dog lying down and you sitting close by on a chair we are going to teach them that they just need to settle.

Don't look directly at your dog, just look over the top of them or out of the corner of your eye, don't speak to them or interact with them other than dropping treats at their hip.

This is the one exercise where we don't want the dog to pay attention to us (or to anything else).

If your dog is looking at you, ignore them, if they get up, guide them into the down with your hand again quietly and drop a treat by their hip so that they roll onto one hip and are in the relaxed position again.

Step three:

Once their attention is not on you and they are relaxed drop another treat by their hip.

Step four:

Repeat this each time they relax and settle, only treating them for chilling out. The trick here is to reward the dog for relaxing and not having their attention directly on you (or anything else in particular).

If they stare at you, ignore them, if they get up, guide them into the down with your hand and start again from the beginning.

Step five:

Keep doing this until you can get them to be relaxed for ten seconds without moving to get up.

Then throw a treat slightly to the side so they have to get up to get it (don't forget they are on a lead so just a few inches away is enough).

Step six:

Get up and give them a walk around and then repeat again (don't forget if they struggle with the next step, go back a step and try again).

Moving on:

Now we have the dog learning to settle next to us we are going to increase the time we ask them to stay settled

Step seven:

Increase the time they are in the settle slowly, making sure to drop treats by their hip to encourage them to stay in that relaxed position

Once you can say 'settle' and point to where you want the dog to settle, then we can start to fade out the treats

Ask your dog to 'settle' and give a treat at near their hip, now start to build up the length of time between the treats

Step eight:

Once you have the 'settle' you can now invite someone else to sit with you and tell them to ignore the dog completely, build up to having a chat, reading a paper or book with your dog will stay relaxed by your feet

Go to bed

Go to bed is a great cue and one that I find is so handy when I just need five minutes without a dog under my feet, you know your doing the washing up and the dog is constantly wandering around under your feet, it's also great for when you want to relax watching the television or when the doorbell rings it has so many uses!

Firstly I want to explain that this cue is at no point a punishment, this is not a 'you have done something I really dislike, off to bed you go' cue, it is a cue to ask your dog to relax (it's also not the same as the chill out cue).

Your dog's bed is somewhere where they can go to sleep, relax and generally rest, it could be a dog bed or a crate it all depends on what you prefer to use, for me it means I want them to go and lie down on their blanket

How to teach your dog go to bed:

Step one:

Firstly, we are going to show our dogs that their bed is one of the best places to be, it's comfy and when they are there good things happen.

Start in a room where there are no distractions and make sure you have plenty of treats.

Put your dog's bed next to you and lure the dog onto the bed with a treat in your hand, as soon as they are on the bed, ask for the down (if they are struggling to go down with just a verbal cue you can go back for now to using your hand signal again as well as the word 'down').

When they are lying down on their bed, feed them 3 treats one after another, then throw a treat to the side so they get off the bed ready to try again.

Repeat x 3

Step two:

Next move a little way away from the dog's bed and repeat the first step guiding them to the bed, asking for the down and then feeding 3 treats one after another

Repeat x 3

Throw a treat to the side to get them off the bed

Step three:

Keep increasing the distance between you and the bed until you are about five steps away from the bed

Repeat x 3

(Give your dog a break)

Next time start the exercise from the beginning again but only do each stage once to remind them what they learnt earlier (if they can't do a step go back one and try again).

We want to ensure we make the bed a nice and calm place to be and only reward for lying down calmly.

Step four:

Now start to increase the distance between the bed and dog. They now have to go two steps themselves to the bed and so on until they can do it from across the room and eventually from another room but take this slowly and don't rush them.

Step five:

When the dog is on the bed lying down, we are now going to increase the time before we give them a treat.

Count to 2 and then go and give three treats one after another whilst they remain in the down, relaxed on their bed.

Then count to 4, 6, 8 and so on (if at any point they get off the bed, guide them back to it and start again).

We are not looking for a stay or a wait here, we are just looking for the dog to relax and this can take time. Once you have built up the time they will relax on their bed, you can offer them a chew on their bed to relax with.

Step six:

Now each time you ask your dog to go to bed you can vary the levels of reward, and start to fade them out. Offer two treats instead of three, then one. Then start to ask for them to go to bed and don't give a treat every time

Stay

There may be times when we need our dog to stay where they are and not move such as a broken glass on the floor and we can't get them to another room or put them somewhere safe (imagine the glass being in their path to the other room).

Teaching the stay is one of the slowest exercises you and your dog will learn, do not rush it. A good stay can take years to perfect and only moments to lose!

Step one:

Ask your dog for a sit or a down (these are the easiest positions to start with), with your dog in the sit or down stand directly in front of your dog. Feed your dog one treat after another x 10 (yep you read that correctly!). Throw a treat to the side to get them to move position so you can start again

Step two:

Now build up very slowly the distance you are away from your dog, making sure to give your marker word before going back to them each time to reward with a treat and then give your release word when you are next to your dog - no more than one step at a time, and if that is too much just lean back slightly or move a foot and build up that way, slowly slowly is the best with stays!

Make sure you practice this lot and only move on to the next step when your dog can stay 5 times in a row without getting up once and do this for three separate sessions in a row.

Step three:

We are only going to move onto the next step when they can stay in position whilst you move away and come back to reward them (they shouldn't move until you give the release word).

Don't rush! If after a week you can only go half a step away, that's fine, build it up slowly (it's worth it), this is really hard for your dogs to learn, we need to build their confidence of being left in a position whilst we move away.

Note: This is different to the 'wait' such as the one we use with door manners where we then ask the dog to come to us or with us. With the stay, they stay in position until we go back to them, never call a dog out of a stay, always go to them and release them from there!

Vier

Chapter Fifteen

Power up your training

Release cue

A release cue tells your dog that they can now move and do their own thing until you ask them to do something else. It's a cue that we don't use for anything else, its only purpose is to tell the dog they are free.

Using a word that you find easy to remember is best and one that comes naturally to you, I use 'OK' but you could use 'Free' or any other word you just need to make sure you are consistent

We only use release cues once the dog fully understands what each exercise is, not before!

Each time you ask your dog to do something (we will use the sit here as an example) we then give the release cue to let the dog know they can move.

Ask your dog to sit, say 'Yes' and reward.

Next time ask your dog to sit, this time instead of saying 'Yes' and rewarding straight away, we are going to wait a few seconds and then say 'Yes' and reward whilst they are still in that position.

Then we are going to say 'OK' and throw a treat to the side for them to go and repeat this 5 times. Then give your dog a break and have another go in the next session

Fading out hand signals

When we first start to train our dogs a new cue the easiest and quickest way is to use a treat in our hand and to lure them into the new position, and to give a hand signal. Over time we want to be able to start to fade this hand signal out so that we can just use our voice.

How do I do fade out my hand signal?

First of all, we need to make sure that we have taught the dog the behaviour we want to see, for ease let's start with the 'sit'.

Your dog now understands that as your hand comes up, their bum goes down and when their bum is on the floor you say 'yes' and reward them with a treat. They also know that when you say 'sit' this means bum on the floor.

Now that they know what 'sit' means and they can do this when you say the word 'sit' and bring your hand up we can start to remove the hand signal. We want to teach them that when you say 'sit' this means bum on the floor even when you don't bring your hand up for them to follow.

Imagine you're carrying a cup of tea in one hand and your phone in the other, you want the dog to sit and wait for a moment whilst you go through the door, it's going to be hard to use a hand signal as your hands are full, this is where a verbal cue really comes in handy.

Also, if they are some way away from you, you want to be able to give the cue with your voice.

Fading

Start off as you have been, asking the dog to 'sit' with your verbal cue and then raising your hand as if you have a piece of string from their nose so that their head comes up and their bum goes down into a sit.

If they get it right say 'yes' and reward them with a treat.

Next, we are going to make the hand signal smaller than before but only just.

Take your hand and imagine your piece of string from their nose and shorten it

- Each time they get it right with a smaller hand signal say 'Yes' and reward with a treat. Repeat x 3
- Keep shortening the sequence of the hand signal until you can just use the verbal cue 'sit'.

If they get it right the first time just the verbal cue, jackpot them with their rewards. Then repeat and go back to a normal reward rate for the first 10 times they do it straight off from the verbal cue.

Then start to randomise your rewards. In future just use your verbal cue

Notes to remember:

Each time we shorten the hand signal, we are looking to fade its use. Don't forget, if they don't sit or they get it wrong, or just look at you blankly, go back a step and start again. If they can't do it twice in a row, go back a step. Make sure you repeat each step at least 3 times.

Don't worry you can still use the hand signal if you want to afterwards (make sure they understand the verbal cue first and can do this reliably and mix it up so they understand that either the hand signal (with no treat in your hand) or the verbal cue of 'sit'.

Extinction burst

Great! You have worked so hard on your dog jumping up, barking, chewing and teaching them all these new cues it's all been going so great!

But wait!!!!

That wonderful new behaviour is now a distant memory and they are worse than they were in the first place, it's like they have forgotten everything you have taught them!

Don't panic!

This is what we call an extinction burst.

The new behaviour is still there, but they are now testing the waters to see if it really does pay off.

That behaviour you thought you had seen the last of is back and back with a vengeance. This is where you MUST be consistent, this is going to be hard but trust me its worth it!

An extinction burst is when the behaviour we don't want to see gets worse before it gets better or after it has got better. The dog has stopped being rewarded for that behaviour and so we have put that behaviour on an extinction schedule, by not rewarding the behaviour it will start to become extinct (not quite like dinosaurs but you get the drift).

The dog then realises that hey I clearly haven't been jumping up high enough, or with enough energy, I must try harder! If I keep going and really make an effort with my jumping up they will notice me and I will get my reward!

They are testing to see if the old behaviour will still elicit a response from you, the problem being if it does it's going to be soooo much harder than before to stop this behaviour.

Think of it this way, when you were up in your room as a teen (yep we have all been there) and you shouted Mom! She didn't reply as she was sick of hearing you shout at her instead of just coming down the stairs! You shout Mom! Mooooom! Mooooooooom! Mom! Mom! Mom! (Or Dad or any other name). You get their attention whoop! Mission accomplished and next time you knew you just had to hang in there longer or be louder!

This is what your dog is doing, they know the behaviour used to work and work well, so if they keep doing it again and keep working at doing it eventually you will give in and voila they have been rewarded for that behaviour!

This is why you need to be uber consistent in your approach, if you reward this old behaviour just once that's it they know it works!

Love my big red bone!

Chapter Sixteen

What's next? Time for you!

Time for you is really important. It's as important as spending time with your dog, we can't always be with our dogs and we need to make sure that they are comfortable being left on their own or having a time out.

It's really important if you haven't already started training your dog to be able to settle and relax and that your dog can do the same.

Two really good exercises to work on here during the day are chill or settle and then go to bed as you found earlier in the book, along with the crate training.

Some dogs don't like to be on their own, if they aren't in the middle of the entertainment they feel like they are missing out. We need to teach them that being on their own and having their own time out is just as much fun as being with us.

Make a note of your score below, how many of these ring true for you?

- Your dog sleeps on your bed or next to your bed or at the very least in the bedroom with you

- Your dog sits and waits for you outside of the bathroom or even goes in the bathroom with you
- Your dog sits and watches or jumps up, howls, whines, barks etc when you are eating
- Your dog follows you from room to room
- If you pop out when you back in the house the dog goes crazy to see you (and you them)
- Your dog goes everywhere with you, to the point that if the dog can't go you don't go!
- Making plans with friends? They must include the dog
- The dog is fed, walked, has play time (everything) before you
- The dog eats better than you do
- The dog has more toys than Harrods!
- If the dog goes out to toilet you go with them (after all they may be scared going out on their own)
- You talk to your dog more than any other person in the household
- Your dog is your furry child
- You rank your dog above an other significant adults in the home

Chances are you have at least ticked off two or more of the above and you know what that is fine, what works for you and your dog is what is best for you and your dog!

The only thing I would say is that, that's a LOT of pressure on a dog.

Don't get me wrong I am guilty of a lot of these as well, it's hard not to be!

But we also need to remember that all this attention and all this time together can make things fraught. Imagine living with someone who never stops talking to you in another language, every time you try to sleep they bother you (hey you're so damn cute!)

Joking aside, it is exhausting for our dogs. It's no wonder every so often they play up, get fed up with us or carry on like they can't be without us for even one minute......we have trained them to be that way!

So yep, take time for you and give your dog time for them, setting aside time away from each other each and every day will really help you both to have a calmer, more enjoyable time and don't forget when you spend time away from each other you really appreciate the time you're together!

Ezekiel as a fully qualified Assistance Dog!

You did it!

Well done for sticking with it, it's not an easy time for you or your dog but after reading this book and putting in the hard work you are well on your way to having a calmer, well behaved dog in your life.

The aim of this book was never to change your dog but to help you to understand them and for them to learn how to behave and what will be rewarded.

The aim of the book however was to change YOU and how you interact with your tenacious teen to get the best results for you both.

Having a tenacious teen is bloody hard work but you did it! And guess what when you get to the other side, you will look back on these days with smiles and laughter at the antics your dog goes up to.

It may take some time but you will look back fondly on these days and eventually who knows you may even choose to go through it all again with another dog!

Good luck ;)

If you would like to support other dogs to help their humans like me as an assistance dog check out DOG A.I.D. **www.dogaid.org.uk**

Me & Dad (2000AD Brit Cit Judge)

Further reading

You glutton for punishment, you want to read more! Well fantastic! That's one of the best ways to learn (and the more we know the more we know there is to learn)

Below are some of the books I recommend to my clients (to be honest with you any titles by these authors are well worth a read!)

The Culture Clash Jean Donaldson

The Other End of the Leash Patricia McConnell

Don't Shoot The Dog! Karen Pryor

The Genius of Dogs Brian Hare

Another Pup Sarah Roper

Puppy Prepared Sarah Roper

The Complete Pupstar Guide Sarah Roper

Forever Dog Rodney Habib & Dr Karen Shaw Becker

And off we go with the next tenacious
teen!

Want more?

Who doesn't love a freebie! To get access to your free bonuses pop over to www.mooofadog.co.uk

Looking for a trainer?

If you are looking for a trainer but I am a bit too far away have a look at the below sites to help you find a local trainer or behaviourist.

Kennel Club Accredited Instructor
www.thekennelclub.org.uk

Animal Behaviour and Training Council
www.abtc.org.uk

The Canine Behaviour and Training Society
www.tcbts.co.uk

Index

Ethel

About the Author

Lillie lives in the heart of the Black Country in the West Midlands, England.

A fully accredited dog training instructor with the Kennel Club, Animal Behaviour & Training Council, The Canine Behaviour and Training Society and International Society of Animal Professionals.

Lillie specialises in adolescent dogs, nervous dogs and assistance dogs.

If not out training one of her own five dogs or out with clients you will find her studying many different areas of dog behaviour and training, or out driving her Traditional Gypsy Cob Ethel in their four wheel carriage.

Printed in Great Britain
by Amazon

77016393R00132